Two Are Better

Midlife Newlyweds Bicycle Coast to Coast

Tim & Debbie Bishop

OPEN
ROAD
PRESS

Publisher's Note

This publication is designed to provide entertainment and inspiration, as well as helpful information about the subject matter covered. It is sold with the understanding that the publisher is not engaged in rendering professional bicycle touring services or professional counseling services. If expert assistance is required, the service of an appropriate professional should be sought. There is no guarantee that hyperlinks on ebook versions will work as intended. The publisher and authors are not responsible for viruses, malware, or other computer scripts that may alter or destroy computer data. Readers who click on hyperlinks do so at their own risk. The publisher and authors are making no endorsements or representations that products mentioned herein or referred to by hyperlink will meet the readers' requirements or expectations.

Contents

Foreword

Creating a new beginning can spark hope, enthusiasm, and confidence!

IN 1944, IN THE MIDST OF A WORLD WAR, the president of Oxford University opened his message to the entering freshman by saying: *"All beginnings are hopeful."* This is a concept that we have seen confirmed throughout history in many different settings. In working with people going through change, I am often presented first with the discouragement, frustration, and frequent anger and resentment of feeling trapped or stuck. I have come to recognize, however, that those feelings always tell me the person is looking backward, at something that has already occurred. As soon as we are able to create a clear plan for the future, those feelings quickly begin to dissipate and are replaced by hope, optimism, enthusiasm, and confidence. In all my years of life coaching, I have never seen a person who has clear plans and goals for the future who is also depressed. They just don't go together.

And in all my years of coaching, I have seldom seen the explosion of hope, optimism, enthusiasm, and confidence shown by Tim Bishop as he entered a new season of his life at fifty-one years old. While his conservative and consistent nature was readily displayed by his work and life history, he, at least verbally, seemed eager to explore options for a new chapter in his life. And, wow, he confirmed that desire with a clear plan and the willingness to act.

Plans quickly developed to leave his twenty-six-year corporate career, to move out of his simple place of living, to get married, and to celebrate his honeymoon with a cross-country bicycle trip—and to pursue a deeper involvement with his favorite ministry. Not only did he wish and dream, he "took action" to see those plans come to life.

With enticing descriptions of the view from a bicycle, Tim and Debbie describe how they unplugged from their old lives, learning how to build a meaningful existence together and to take a fresh look at what was truly important.

With humor and candor, they present a challenge for each of us: are we too busy with our daily lives to really explore our purpose for being alive? From the book: "What interests, abilities, passions, and gifts do we have? How can we use these to fulfill our purpose? What goals can we set that will move us closer to achieving our purpose? What boundaries on our relationships and our time are appropriate to achieve these goals? Is it time for a fresh start in 'real' life?"

I encourage you to read this book with new eyes—to be willing to consider what a fresh start would look like for you. I strongly suspect that Tim and Debbie's story will inspire you to reevaluate your own life story and to add your own elements of new meaning and purpose. Enjoy the journey!

Dan Miller
Author and Life Coach
www.48Days.com

Preface

DID YOU EVER NOTICE that some things take an inordinate amount of time? Our pursuit of finding that special lifelong companion took fifty-two years. Most people take their first stab at it by twenty or thirty; some get it wrong and have had a few repeat tries by the time they reach forty. Others, of course, never marry or don't care to. Regardless, many people agree that two are better than one. Like one of the wisest men ever—King Solomon of ancient times—said,

> *Two are better than one,*
> *Because they have a good reward for their labor.*
> *For if they fall, one will lift up his companion.*
> *But woe to him who is alone when he falls,*
> *For he has no one to help him up.*
> *Again, if two lie down together, they will keep warm;*
> *But how can one be warm alone?*
> *Though one may be overpowered by another, two can*
> *   withstand him.*
> *And a threefold cord is not quickly broken.*
>
> —Ecclesiastes 4:9-12

Beautiful, isn't it? Something within the human heart longs for companionship, as if life itself hinges upon finding that elusive puzzle piece.

Life has its own agenda, its sands of time no respecter of people, circumstances, events, disappointments, heartbreaks, or tragedies. The complexity of life, with its challenging relationships, vacillating emotions, and petty details, can obscure the incessant ticking of its clock. Before you know it, you have simply begun to drift with the winds of routine that define everyday life.

One day, though, the alarm sounds, rousing you from a deep sleep. You awaken to realize you have arrived at an unintended "place," one no longer healthy, one not where you are called to be. Monotony had dropped by uninvited and, like company that overstays its welcome, refused to leave, stealing away passion, discovery, and growth. What once was fresh, stimulating, and exciting faded away while you were looking in the other direction. Sometimes, you need to change course to reinvigorate life and reawaken what you have to bring to the world around you. Debbie and I resolved to do just that—first my retirement, and then marriage. And as our first step as a married couple, why not pursue another dream of a lifetime: bicycling coast to coast?

We have chosen a co-authoring approach to sharing our story. After all, two are better than one. I (Tim) am the black-ink narrator, while Debbie weighs in with her indented, magenta comments. As we share our glorious journey in the pages that follow, you can expect several things. First, this is a celebration—a celebration of love and life, a celebration of the beauty of our land, and a celebration of God's blessings. You will find fun, adventure, love, pictures of interesting and beautiful places, and a challenge to the human spirit. This is also a story that describes how good things happen to those who wait, how God's very goodness is unveiled as we step out in faith. We think you will also agree that life is more enjoyable and fulfilling when shared with someone you love.

You will also learn what a cross-country bicycle tour is like. And you may conclude that you, too, can bicycle coast to coast! You can choose to do so vicariously by reading along, or you may plan to do so yourself and thus glean some interesting and useful information about the experience.

Regardless of your interest in bicycling, we hope you are inspired to embark on your own journey, to reinvigorate your own life, and to pursue your own dreams, whatever they may be. But don't wait too long, for time stands still for no one. Decide today to move! On second thought, finish the book first. And please enjoy the ride!

1. Getting Started

EVERY STORY HAS A BEGINNING. Ours starts on April 22, 2010, just eight days before my retirement from a twenty-six-year career in the corporate world. There we were, atop Cadillac Mountain in Acadia National Park. What had taken decades was finally beginning to unfold with the words, "Will you marry me?" *Wow,* I thought. *I have always wanted to say that. I wonder what this will be like.* Debbie, a literacy specialist in Massachusetts, and that unique, God-chosen other half of me, accepted my proposal. Life was about to change at breakneck speed.

One thing was immediately clear to both of us. There was no need for an extended engagement. Fifty-two years had been long enough to wait. We soon set our wedding date for June 19.

I have also always wanted to bicycle across America. As it turned out, so had Debbie. In fact, her 1994 list of things to accomplish before she dies said so. Moments after our magical engagement, still atop Cadillac Mountain, we broached the idea of a cross-country bicycle trip as an extended honeymoon, an adventure to celebrate the union of two lifelong singles with birthdays only fifteen days

One adventure leads to another two weeks later

1

apart. Life was about to begin in earnest. Was there any reason to put off such a grand way to celebrate our newfound gift? The shackles were off—and we had a lot of catching up to do. What better way to get started?

Within a couple of weeks, it became clear that cycling coast to coast was not just a passing fancy. We were both interested and serious about the adventure. Could we make it all the way across the country before Debbie's return to work in late August? And, with both of us fifty-two years old, could we even make it across the state of Oregon, let alone the Rocky Mountains? If we made it that far, how much time would it take to ride the next 3,000 miles?

Frankly, completing the trek seemed trivial at the time. We were embarking on the ultimate getaway for not only bicycling enthusiasts, but also a much larger populous. Haven't most people ridden a bicycle as a child and fantasized about the freedom of the open road? We would worry about the details later. Certainly, there would be plenty of airports sprinkled along our route, wherever that would take us. We were not going to deny ourselves this opportunity. We decided to pursue it with reckless abandon—and with a new companion by our side: one another!

What ensued over the next several weeks was nothing short of amazing. In just two months, we would be husband and wife, pedaling bicycles and carrying items needed for our journey, most of which we had not yet purchased, all the way across the country. And, before we left, I would vacate my apartment of twenty-five years, sorting through my belongings and placing into storage those worth keeping. From scratch, we would determine our wishes and needs for both a wedding and a cross-country bicycle ride. Debbie's teaching obligations ended two days before our wedding. Thankfully, I could now dedicate myself full-time to prepare for both events. We would worry about the rest of our lives later!

2. Our Story

TO APPRECIATE THE SIGNIFICANCE of our coast-to-coast bicycle trip and the life to follow, you first need to hear another story. What was it that brought two fifty-two-year-old lifelong singles together? We shared some significant passions yet lived hundreds of miles apart. Well, if you are suspecting the Internet, you understand only a small part of the story.

Longsuffering

On New Year's Eve of the new millennium, I had vowed in a church service to entrust my desire for a husband to God, denouncing an old approach that left me emotionally bruised and empty. I still longed for companionship, but I wasn't going to obsess about it. I had made a decision to reinvent my life in 1996. After twenty years in Colorado, I moved to New England with neither a job nor a place to live. I'd had a strong impression that God would answer my prayers for a husband after moving East. I went back to school for my master's degree, began work as a literacy specialist, and discovered the benefits of a commitment to a local church.

Like Debbie, I had endured years of loneliness, even while enjoying blessings in other aspects of life. I had forever been praying for a companion, or so it seemed. Everything within me and around me—what I had learned as a child, observed in others, learned from the Bible, and experienced in my own life—told me that God would provide a special companion. However, it seemed so elusive for so long. Finally, I became so tired of praying about it that I tried to focus more on enjoying what I already had. Work became both a blessing and a curse. It filled time with interesting and productive activity. I enjoyed it and excelled at it, but it proved to be an inadequate substitute for the love that the right woman could offer.

Despite the frustration of my unfulfilled desire, I still longed for that special someone to complete me.

Journey into Cyberspace

As our parallel longing for companionship intensified, Debbie and I decided to use the Internet to help locate prospective mates. Because I was leery about whom I might meet online, I was merely looking for a casual friendship. I could always assess further potential once I became better acquainted with the more promising women.

So, in 2003, we met on a website that we had each tried for only a month. Since Debbie's one-month trial membership was free, I will always be able to remind her that she got what she paid for. But, then again, I only paid $10 to discover her. There she was, with username "JoyfulDebbie," coyly snuggled next to a statue, sporting her cute dimples, sassy short hairdo, and Colorado ski sweater. *This looks interesting,* I thought.

> My decision to go online followed several years of growing spiritually and personally. After some intense schoolwork and beginning a new job, I was looking for some fun—meaning a Christian man who loved bicycling, skiing, and hiking. But I was hoping for a serious relationship, too.
>
> When I first saw Tim's profile online, there wasn't much to look at—well, what I mean is, he didn't post a photo. But, because he enjoyed bicycling and lived close by, in Maine, I decided to consider him further. So, we began corresponding.

In the five years that followed our introduction in cyberspace, Debbie and I spent only a handful of times face to face. Yet, we developed a meaningful and supportive friendship by becoming, in effect, e-mail pen pals. We first met in person for a bicycle ride in Keene, New Hampshire, in 2004. I arrived first at the Monadnock High School parking lot. Moments later, when Debbie zipped in and bounced out of her Toyota Echo, I could see she was well-matched to her small car—at least until I saw her power-lift her bicycle from atop its roof-mounted rack. *Whoa!* I thought. *Is she strong or what?*

When I first saw Tim, I noticed he wasn't wearing the typical biking apparel. As we got to know one another, I could see that this didn't matter much to him—and to me, either. After our ride, we enjoyed a dinner at a Mexican restaurant in town and then parted as friends.

Debbie and I enjoyed our time together in New Hampshire and related well to one another. We had the basis for a good friendship, but there were no instant fireworks. Although we shared an intense passion for both the Christian faith and bicycling, the time was not right for us to come together in a more intimate way.

Our first ride years ago

I had two serious relationships between the fall of 2004 and January 2007. The first man seemed on the surface to possess many of the interests and qualities I was looking for in a husband. In time, however, the relationship soured and ended abruptly, leaving me hurt again. My relationship with the second man seemed destined to fail from the start, but accelerated to a wedding engagement. After listening to the counsel of others and the depth of my own heart, I broke off the engagement and eventually the relationship.

Since we continued to correspond during her two serious relationships, I could see that these painful experiences were preparing Debbie for a deeper and more lasting attachment. She was developing greater emotional security and growing spiritually.

In the meantime, I invested a lot of time on another matching website, processing through literally thousands of so-called matches. Although their program identified these women as compatible with me, a quick review of their profiles made it clear they were not really matches at all.

People who knew me over the years, and even some who did not, had offered advice with the best of intentions, but usually failing to understand my perspective. I hated that. Often, the inference was that I was to blame—it was my fault I was still single. They eventually backed off. I think they began to realize I was adapting to bearing my own cross. Or perhaps I had just stopped sharing my woes, and they had concluded I would always be single and contented with it. I was just thankful when people quit bugging me about it.

Then there were others—and I know Debbie had them, too—who were truly supportive. When heartache and frustration resurfaced and we needed some understanding, they listened well but stopped short of trying to fix a problem they could not control. They then joined us with their own prayers that we would each meet and marry God's best for us.

Work Matters

Aside from our failed, self-managed matchmaking attempts, Debbie and I each lived full and meaningful single lives. We were busy, some might say entrenched. Professionally, we overinvested in our jobs. After years of praying for a compatible companion who loved God, we each wondered whether the possibility of marriage was passing us by. That's not to say we had given up hope, but this was the backdrop leading to the life-changing events that finally began to unfold.

Even as Debbie and I began spending more time together at play, something was also beginning to brew at work. In late 2006, a change in leadership occurred at the top of a company I had worked for since 1983. My long-term boss, a highly respected finance expert with impressive mettle and judgment—and a one-time heir apparent to lead the company—was passed over for the head job in favor of another vice president with a different skill set, demeanor, and persuasion. I can still remember the day of the announcement. The feeling in the pit of my stomach suggested an impending end to a long-term work relationship, one to which I had given untold personal hours and devotion, and for which I had been well compensated. The process, though, took over three years to unfold.

In late summer of 2007, the company hired an individual from outside the industry as its chief financial officer. He had led a large organization in the past and the company wanted to strengthen its senior management for succession planning purposes. The prior CFO had devoted much of his attention to overseeing the company's substantial real estate portfolio. Therefore, in my role as treasurer, I was already functionally overseeing and performing many of the responsibilities expected of my new boss. From my perspective, the introduction of this new CFO suggested that God had something for me elsewhere and was preparing the way for my departure. In fact, I'd had a strong impression when I assumed the treasurer role in 2004 that God was preparing me for something more, stretching me in new ways, adding leadership experience to my already well-developed technical skills.

It would take time to shed the significant responsibilities I had shouldered. At the peak of my responsibility, I managed five mid-level professionals who helped oversee accounting, internal auditing, and information technology for this multimillion-dollar company with more than 1,000 employees. At the same time, I was defining and executing the company's primary commodity hedging program and dealing with a major operational crisis as a board member of a mission-critical joint venture. The company was also undergoing significant and long overdue changes to its back office systems. It was a stressful time, one that took a significant toll on my ever-shrinking personal life. But it was also an exciting, fast-moving time.

In order for my future to unfold both professionally and personally, I would need to let go. The deep ties and great experiences I'd had with this company would not make the process easy. Like a parent whose children someday leave home, I would need to accept that change was imminent. In effect, both functionally from the company's perspective and emotionally from my own, I had become stuck. It would be some time before I could break free.

There can be both a false sense of security and an unhealthy dependency on money when embedded in a long-term job. Sometimes, you can grow and mentor others, sometimes you can become too comfortable, and sometimes you can reach a dead end where the flame of your drive, knowledge, influence, and enthusiasm diminishes to a flicker before it fizzles out. I had experienced all of these phases, but my flicker was about to become utterly quenched. Circumstances change and we change—or we should. Sometimes, the human psyche struggles to catch up, to recognize growth has stopped, and to muster the courage to move on. I slowly came to appreciate that unlimited options await those who are willing to take a risk. As the new CFO acclimated to the company, a long transition period ensued. Others were being equipped for functions that would ultimately pave the way for my departure.

Friendship Blossoms

In December 2007, Debbie and I celebrated our fiftieth birthdays after the official dates had already lapsed. I drove to Massachusetts and, after a bowling outing, took Debbie to Harvard Square for the premiere of a movie entitled *What Would Jesus Buy?* I thought, *This will be fun. I've never been to a premiere showing before.*

> Tim and I had now reached the official age of maturity—and maturity comes with its advantages. We qualified for our first senior citizen discounts. But I have to admit, I was rather insulted when they didn't ask me to verify my age.

When we walked into the theater, we saw only about thirty people amidst a multitude of empty seats. We then watched the satirically orchestrated spoof on shopping in America, complete with a white-suited evangelist, his tour bus, and his choir. Although I'd seen better movies, I had never been to one where the lead actor visited us in person after the show.

A late-night meal capped off a unique, enjoyable, and memorable evening. Sometime after midnight, I headed north and stayed at a motel en route to Maine. It had been great to see Debbie again and share in our common milestone, but we still had our separate lives. We returned to them while continuing to stay in contact through e-mail.

Having a guy who just wanted to be friends was a new concept to me. I felt comfortable and safe with Tim. Because the emphasis was on friendship, we established trust early in our relationship. There was no pressure, no need to impress—just two fifty-year-olds enjoying each other's company.

In 2004, I had purchased a condominium at an inopportune time. While conventional wisdom told me home ownership was a wise investment, the real estate market collapsed in 2008. Like countless other unsuspecting homeowners, I saw the value of my condominium fall below my purchase price and my mortgage balance. To make matters worse, I needed to use credit cards to bridge an unintended cash deficit. I then took a second job waiting tables to meet my financial obligations. An active social life became a casualty.

As difficult as this experience was, it really put some perspective around the illusory "American dream." In fact, it shattered the dream. I became a slave to this so-called dream as I wrestled to free myself from its grip. Work came to define my day-to-day existence. I realized I needed to manage my finances better. I had my home, but the baggage that came with it changed how I would view it in the future. The American dream is not all that people think it is.

As Debbie was coming to terms with her financial woes, I watched from the sidelines and continued my own struggles with a challenging situation at work. Although I wondered about Debbie's cash crunch, I also could see she wasn't standing idly by feeling sorry for herself. Instead, exercising honesty, humility, and hard work, she recognized a problem, sought help and counseling, and worked to free herself. I had always enjoyed Debbie's company. She was fun and brought joy to our times together. We also shared common spiritual beliefs that accentuated our comfort level. But, now, she had earned my respect.

I wanted to understand whether God might be bringing us together as more than just friends. I struggled to understand how to get to know her better when she lived so many miles away.

I wondered what she would be like if we spent larger blocks of time together. Being good friends is one thing, but experiencing everyday life in close quarters is quite another.

Debbie and I had been enjoying a slow, evolving friendship, which was refreshing despite the distance that separated us. But her victorious living convinced me to commit more of myself to our friendship. So, as our friendship continued to blossom, our visits soon became a monthly occurrence. Over the next two years, we racked up some travel expenses to get to know one another better while honoring our commitment to God and our gift to ourselves to remain pure until marriage.

Growing Closer

In July of 2008, Tim invited me to Maine and agreed to act as my tour guide to Acadia National Park. I had always wanted to visit Acadia based on testimonials from adventuresome friends. In fact, it was on my list of things to do before I die. I readily accepted Tim's offer.

Despite a "Rocky Mountain high" from a recent visit to Colorado, the beauty of Acadia overwhelmed me. Our bicycle rides through the park were fantastic. Not only did we enjoy bicycling, we took the elevator to the top of the Penobscot Narrows Observatory overlooking Penobscot Bay, watched the sunset atop Cadillac Mountain, dined at the Jordan Pond House, and walked the streets of Bar Harbor and along the water one night. It was the most romantic two days I ever spent with, well, a friend!

Bar Harbor marks the official end of Adventure Cycling's Northern Tier cross-country bicycle route. Little did we know that we would be following that route on our honeymoon two years later!

My heart fluttered at Debbie's enthusiastic display of affection when she dashed across the parking lot and greeted me with a resounding hug. It was wonderful to have an attractive and athletic female friend who enjoyed some of the same energetic activities

I liked. *Someone like this does not come along every day!* I thought.

One of our activities began as a delightful tandem ride through the carriage paths of Acadia. As storm clouds approached, I couldn't understand why she wanted to stop—until we did. Her seat was swiveling loosely on its post. There was no quick fix—it wasn't as if I carried a wrench in my back pocket, and we were still miles from the bicycle rental shop. So, despite Debbie's pleas for relief, I said, "Just deal with it!"

> I couldn't believe he said that. Then the sky lit up, the thunder boomed, and the rain clouds opened, prompting a drenching dash back to the shop. Regardless, it was a joyous time of laughing in the rain. After the ride, the sun returned. Sometimes, even the downpours of life can bring blessing with the right perspective, especially when shared with a friend. And one can only hope those downpours are short-lived.

After a sun- and fun-filled couple of days, I was destined for my annual trek to Soulfest, a four-day, outdoor Christian rock festival in New Hampshire. I invited Debbie, but she had another commitment. I was disappointed. But I was also accustomed to attending this event solo and was just thankful for the memory of the past two days. That night, a friend urged Debbie to change her plans. When an online search identified an available motel room near the concert venue, she decided to come. Our extended time together produced wonderful memories before she returned to her summer job two days later. One highlight of this trip was getting caught in another downpour. It was a highlight because we only had one small umbrella.

Another facet of our long-distance relationship that helped assess compatibility and

Enjoying Soulfest together

calling was an e-mail study of the book of Ecclesiastes. True to form, Debbie enthusiastically embraced the study. I assigned the reading and questions. We traded answers after each lesson.

Our self-paced study took well over a year and had a powerful impact. Debbie's transparent responses thrilled me. We were connecting like kindred spirits. The book of Ecclesiastes suggests that much of what we do in life, particularly in work, is meaningless in the grand scheme. This resonated with me as I grappled with issues at work. Other strong themes from our study became evident, as well: Two people working together are better than one. The vigor we have for life, if not life itself, ends quickly, so one should not waste time. And, if one waits for perfect conditions, opportunity will slip by.

In August 2008, I took my mother on a vacation that reached from Maine to Virginia. On the way back to Maine, we met Debbie for ice cream near her home. After we parted, Mom said, "I can see why you like her!" Debbie and I met halfway in September to participate in the Seacoast Century bicycle ride, where well over 1,500 participants bicycle 100 miles from New Hampshire into Maine and Massachusetts, all in one day. Then, in October, Debbie's father and sister accompanied her to Maine for a short vacation, which provided me an opportunity to become acquainted with some of her family.

A memorable trip in November 2008 exemplified the extent of our enjoyable yet exhausting courtship. I traveled south to Debbie's on a Friday after work, a five-hour trip. On Saturday morning, I picked Debbie up for a ninety-minute trip to Rhode Island to watch a college football game on a rainy day. After the game, we headed to Bridgeport, Connecticut, some two hours to the west, to watch five Christian bands in concert in an event called Rock the Sound. The headline group was a favorite of ours, the Newsboys. When the concert concluded late in the evening, we headed back to Debbie's, which was about two and a half hours away. I checked into my motel that evening around two thirty in the morning! The next day, we attended church before I headed back to Maine. I get tired now just thinking about it, but it was great fun and energizing at the time. We were having a blast!

Over the holidays, Debbie came to Maine to visit. It was on this trip, she reminds me, that we first kissed. We continued to connect regularly. In April 2009, we were in Houlton, Maine, for Easter. This was Debbie's first visit to the place where I grew up and to my mother's home. Debbie and Mom quickly developed an affinity for one another. Since my mother knew me very well and had been praying for years for a godly wife for me, this was a strong endorsement. By springtime, Debbie and I had committed to ride in the annual bike-a-thon for a Christian school in Houlton, and we were getting together on weekends to train. In early June, we went back to Houlton to ride the fundraiser's 100-mile course.

Decision-Making

Although we both wanted a spouse, I did not have a peace about accelerating the pace. There was too much uncertainty and chaos at work. I had also witnessed Debbie's last relationship, which suggested to me that slower was better.

> The closer together Tim and I grew emotionally, the more anxious I was becoming. I began to believe he was never going to make a commitment. I kept asking him, "Where is this going?" These inquiries only seemed to annoy him.
>
> To allay my fears, God confronted me twice with the following verse:
>
> > But those who wait on the Lord
> > Shall renew their strength;
> > They shall mount up with wings like eagles,
> > They shall run and not be weary,
> > They shall walk and not faint.
> > — Isaiah 40:31
>
> Tim had just revealed how God had shown him that verse fourteen years earlier. God had not forgotten us. I needed to put my hope in the Lord. I knew that to wait was to honor God. Yet, waiting was so difficult.

In July 2009, Debbie flew to Nashville to help her father liquidate his belongings and move to Denver near her sister. Debbie invited me to help, so I booked a flight and traveled to Tennessee. On a Sunday, Debbie and I attended a local community church. Knowing my struggles already at work, Debbie picked up a *Christian Classifieds* flyer at the church. Later, while traveling back to Bangor, I reviewed the flyer, highlighted some interesting leads, and tucked it away. Meanwhile, Debbie, her sister Ayme, her brother-in-law Mike, and her father were off to Denver with the loaded moving van.

While in the Nashville area, Debbie and I visited TheHopeLine, an organization I have supported for years. We witnessed their central call center in action. Little did we know we would be promoting this nonprofit on a cross-country bicycle trip as husband and wife a year later!

> During our visit to the TheHopeLine, we were talking with the call center manager when a "Hope Coach" interrupted her with a suicide call from a troubled youth. The skill, compassion, and composure with which she handled the crisis left us dumbfounded. She adeptly and lovingly connected the suicidal person with a counselor from an agency that specializes in suicide intervention, and then she calmly resumed our tour. I was so moved that I became a Hope Coach a few months later.

About a month after returning from Nashville, I was at home contemplating my situation at work and a long-distance relationship that was hard to resolve at a distance. I noticed the marked-up *Christian Classifieds* flyer among a pile of papers on my desk. I checked out some of the leads I had highlighted on the plane. One of them led me to a website that marketed some career counseling material. I immediately purchased and read a book entitled *No More Mondays* by Dan Miller. The content of this book resonated with me. It explained how corporate settings could sometimes get the better of you. It was full of encouragement about a way out to a better work life, as well as better balance in all facets of life. Boy, did I ever need that. I was so intrigued that I purchased and read another one of Miller's books, entitled *48 Days to the Work You Love*. This book was more of a conventional career and job-search counseling book, but was replete with the same principles found in the first book, undeniably sound principles that I began to dwell on—and from which there was no escape.

The quest continued. In another month, I was back on the 48days.com website and discovered that Dan Miller was not only an author but also a so-called life coach. *Strange term,* I thought. *Sounds like a way to reel in unsuspecting people and make some money off them, using the Internet as an incredibly strong fishing pole!* However, since Miller espoused Christian principles, I looked further. I reviewed the material on how to request a life coach. Applicants would either be assigned to Miller or, more likely, one of the associates in his network.

Some of the questions on the application really struck me:

- "If the doctor told you today you had six months to live, what would you do in those remaining months?"
- "If you received a $7 million inheritance tomorrow, what would you do? How would your life change?"
- "What are you doing in your life now that will last forever?"
- "In writing your epitaph, what would you want people to remember about you?"

I was already asking myself these same questions. They mirrored themes from our Ecclesiastes study. I knew I was stuck and needed help. I was feeling pressure on multiple fronts—and it was getting to me. At a minimum, I needed some career counseling, and it was important to me that it be from a Christian perspective.

As I considered the questionnaire, I thought, *What have I got to lose—other than some more time?* Therefore, I completed the application and submitted it. Incidentally, in response to the question, "If the doctor told you today you had six months to live, what would you do in those remaining months?" I wrote the following sentence: "This is easy to answer because I just had a similar exercise in a Bible study recently…. I would bike across the United States…perhaps accompanied by a special lady friend."

Beautiful view of the Atlantic Ocean atop Day Mountain in Acadia

As I struggled with my future, Debbie and I continued to grow closer. We had a fantastic ten-day stretch in the summer of 2009, visiting Mom in Houlton, bicycling and sightseeing in Acadia, and the usual mix of bicycling and listening to great music in a beautiful outdoor setting at Soulfest. A few weeks later, in Florida, I met her mother and stepfather for the first time. We rented bicycles and, despite the heat, discovered August is a good time to be bicycling aside the sparse traffic in southern Florida! Thereafter, we continued to connect as we were able, but my sights and decision-making were focused on the conundrum at work.

A couple of weeks after submitting an application for a life coach on the 48days.com website, I was astonished when I received this personal response from Dan Miller himself: "I receive between 150 and 200 coaching requests each month. With my writing commitments, I refer 99% of those to other competent coaches in our 48 Days network, selecting perhaps one or two people with which to engage. And your rich theological and philosophical description of your current situation grabbed my attention as being someone I would love working with personally." This was most flattering to me, but $4,500 was a large price to pay. Questions arose in my mind: *Will I get any benefit? I am asking a total stranger to provide me help, and* *he lives in Tennessee? And, by the way, pay him $4,500?* This required some thought, prayer, and counsel. But after a few more weeks of remaining stuck while I considered the opportunity, I signed on. There was a providential convergence as I left for Tennessee, after Mr. Miller had flexibly and graciously fit me into his busy schedule.

I arrived at his office, adjacent to his residence, to an unlocked door and an unattended facility. Since he had a prior engagement, he had invited me to make myself at home. At the end of the hall was a bedroom with a space heater warming a bed with folded down covers. This was my introduction to his Southern hospitality. After several days at Mr. Miller's "sanctuary," I found him to be not only authentic, but also insightful, intelligent, down-to-earth, caring, and spiritual. He had a firm grasp on my work dilemma and helped me craft a plan that would help determine my future, or at least begin the process of discovering it. Before leaving Tennessee, I was again able to visit with some of the great folks at TheHopeLine, just twenty minutes away from Mr. Miller's office. Coincidence? I don't think so!

The final blows precipitating my job departure came late in 2009. Two senior-level executives, from whom I had received great support and mentoring over the years, chose to retire early. Then the company presented a restructuring plan formalizing a structure in which the company's new CFO assumed full control of the finance department. My diminished role and responsibility simply did not feel right. I had discussions with the company's leadership regarding my future. I presented a handful of potential roles I felt would utilize my strengths to the company's benefit and mine while still respecting the spirit of their restructuring plan. When these concepts were summarily rejected, the time had come to move on. I had no doubt in my mind or heart. As difficult as it was to leave a company that had owned a part of me, indeed had been a part of me, for the past twenty-six years, God had already been making a provision that would make this time the most exciting of my life!

In January 2010, I provided my employer with a three-month notice of my intention to leave the company. My final day would be April 30, 2010. My decision surprised Debbie, despite how open I had been with her throughout the process. As the pressure cooker had intensified at work, she was also adding pressure on the relationship front. She couldn't seem to understand or accept that I was in the midst of a personal crisis—but, apparently, she was in one of her own. She kept asking me where the relationship was going, and I'd had it with that question. We agreed if it came up again, we would take a break.

> I just couldn't take it any longer. I was dying inside, day by day, for a commitment from Tim. He was more concerned about his work than me. I had wanted a spouse for so long and believed God would provide one. Although Tim had never asked for a commitment from me, if I waited indefinitely for him, I was limiting my options because of our deep emotional ties. And if this was only going to be a friendship, I was headed for heartbreak.

Inevitably, that same question came up again: "Where is this going?" We knew we needed a "time-out" (as we called it). I can still remember the moment, both stricken with emotion, falling to her kitchen floor, lying clenched in one another's arms, and sobbing uncontrollably for the better part of an hour. After we had caught our collective breath, I can still remember sitting in her living room, watching the sun beaming in on her lovely but saddened face, and hearing the teary words, "I always wanted to meet a nice Christian man like you." Of all the words she has ever said to me, those pierced me like a knife in the heart. But it was no use—life was at an impasse. I had turmoil within and needed space. I needed the fog to clear. Debbie was ready for commitment, but I was not. Even in parting, we felt and showed for one another the love of true friends. It was unusual and spoke powerfully for the depth of our feelings.

During a three-week hiatus, we were heartsick. I began to be flooded with reasons why I should marry Debbie, ninety-one of them in fact! As a friend put it, this was a gift from God, an answer to prayer. The separation was providing me better clarity on the relationship, even while much uncertainty and lack of clarity existed about my professional future. I began to realize I would never find anyone who fit me better than Debbie. Even though the future was highly uncertain, I realized the embodiment of a goal, a dream, and a blessing was right within my grasp.

> During our time-out, I did have other options, but I didn't want them. I only wanted Tim. No matter what I did, God was still requiring me to wait on Him. Later, after I understood Tim better, I regretted pushing him. He told me he was listening and watching for God to lead him. And that is just what He did. Knowing that Tim was waiting on the Lord really strengthened my trust in him, something I often lacked with other men in the past.

Maybe I'd had this all backward. God wasn't going to lay out my future work first; instead, He was going to fulfill my longing for companionship. I didn't need to have the work piece figured out—that could take years. God was trying to answer a prayer that I, and others, had volleyed around for a long, long time. If Debbie and I were to be together, that could mean a significantly different work model than if I remained single. What might the remainder of my professional life, and hers for that matter, look like if we were one? In effect, God was giving me a choice. I could ask Debbie to marry me or I could begin a new life without her. He could bless either option, but I needed to make a choice—another big decision on the heels of the one I had just made. After years of loneliness, praying, searching, and anguishing, I finally knew deep inside what I really wanted. Consistent with Ecclesiastes 4:9a, I decided that "two are better than one." Debbie was a gift from God—that is, if she would see things the same way. With each of us armed with better clarity, we resumed our relationship while I began the homestretch at work.

One Door Closes While Another Opens

On April 23, the company would sponsor a retirement luncheon in my honor. I wanted Debbie to attend the event to give her a glimpse of my soon-to-be former life. Since it was scheduled during her school vacation week, she agreed to attend. She came to Bangor a couple of days before the event. On April 22, I met her after work and took her to Acadia National Park, just an hour from Bangor. We arrived in time to walk up Cadillac Mountain and watch a beautiful sunset. While the sun was setting in the same location where we had enjoyed wonderful outings in the past two years, I popped the question!

"Will you marry me?"

> I knew leaving work was a big deal for Tim, so I was astounded when he proposed to me the night before his retirement luncheon. I said to him, "Really? You want to marry me?" After I got over the shock, I was elated. That night will forever be etched in my mind—and my heart!

Debbie's immediate, calm, and joyful acceptance of my proposal signaled that the time had been right! The radiance that shone from her beautiful face and the sparkle in her eyes attested to the divine nature of our heavenly moment. Instantly, years of heartache, longing, and waiting had vanished. After years in dry dock, this boat was about to set sail. And it was more than ready!

As the sun dropped from the sky, we agreed we would like to be married soon. We discussed the possibility of a bicycle trip across the United States after our wedding. We also talked about how we would announce our engagement. Since the luncheon the next day would be a great forum to spring some exciting news to a room full of potential well-wishers, we decided to keep our secret for at least a few more hours. My mother and my brother's family would also be attending the luncheon. My mother had told me many years ago that, if I ever was to marry, she did not want to hear about it over the phone. She was about to get her wish!

> As if one surprise wasn't enough, the two that followed suggested that our new status as an engaged couple had already opened up a world of fun and adventure. I had always fantasized about bicycling across the country. I had no idea

An "engaging" sunset over Eagle Lake on April 22, 2010!

what it would take to pull this off in time for a summer trip, but the thought was incredibly intriguing. And when Tim suggested springing our news to the group at the end of his retirement luncheon, it didn't take long to warm up to the idea. I have never been the best one to hold onto a surprise, but this one would be well worth the wait!

Debbie exercised great restraint during the luncheon, although it was difficult to hide the glow on her face. The luncheon was emotional. Many in the room had mixed feelings on my departure, as I had many years with the company and was leaving well before conventional retirement age. One by one, the speakers gave their tributes, in the spirit of both roast and respect. However, I had the last word.

At the end of my difficult and emotional speech, I introduced the guests seated at my table. I introduced my family first and then "my friend Debbie." I continued, "Debbie lives in Massachusetts. She came up Wednesday night. Last night, we were actually able to go down to Bar Harbor after work, and climbed up on top of Cadillac. There was a nice sunset and I asked Debbie if she would marry me!" The pent-up emotion in the room erupted in jubilation. Every person was on his or her feet. The stiff retirement luncheon had checked out in favor of a jubilee with accompanying hug-fest.

> When Tim announced our big secret, I was looking right at his mother, Frannie. She was so overjoyed. My future sister-in-law Marilynn was beside herself. The three of us got up and hugged. It meant so much to see how happy they were. I felt so welcomed into my new family—what an unforgettable moment!

The future looks bright at Tim's retirement luncheon!

As the clamor began to subside, some of the more observant well-wishers shouted over the din, "What did she say?" This was Debbie's prompt to join me at the podium and cheerfully answer, "I said yes!" Thankfully, a colleague shared an audio recording, and so we are able to relive this moment from time to time. It serves as a powerful reminder of God's provision when you most need it and least expect it.

3. A New Day Dawning

FOLLOWING THE RETIREMENT LUNCHEON, Debbie and I headed to Houlton with Mom. Amid the roller coaster of emotions of the prior few days, all three of us tossed and turned through an excited and virtually sleepless night. There was so much to process: the joy of a fantastic sendoff, leaving work and what "retirement" would mean, planning and looking forward to a wedding in the upcoming weeks, and life as a married couple. Then there was the cross-country bicycle ride. Was it feasible this summer, could we handle it, and what would we encounter? And, of course, where would we eventually live? But this day was all about the ecstasy of the celebration. One thing was for sure: life had changed—thank goodness.

The following week was my last at work. I recalled voluntarily leaving my first professional job thirty years earlier. During my final walk out the door on that day, strong, uncontrollable emotions overtook me unsuspectingly. This time, again much to my surprise, no tears came when walking out for the last time—rather, I felt a sense of peace. I had made the right decision. Although my professional future was uncertain, surely there was a bright future ahead.

> My colleagues at school held a bridal shower in my honor. I had attended so many of these fun events, and had nearly lost hope I would ever have one of my own. It was wonderful. My creative peers outfitted me with a bicycle helmet, adorned with a bridal veil, and sequin-trimmed bicycling gloves! To accentuate the camping theme, they placed gifts inside a pup tent and toasted marshmallows on an open campfire—all in the school playground!

So much had happened in such a short period. I had questions about whether a new job opportunity would arise for me in Maine, where I had lived most of my life. I notified my landlord I would be leaving my small, one-bedroom apartment of twenty-five years. It would simply not be large enough to fit our belongings, and Debbie had no immediate intentions of leaving her teaching job in Massachusetts. We soon concluded that a bicycle adventure across the continent following our wedding in June would be a fantastic, once-in-a-lifetime opportunity. Setting the wedding date and booking a plane flight set immovable deadlines for the flurry of planning and activity about to unfold. Included in the pre-wedding activities were several remote marriage counseling sessions with two pastors in different parts of Maine. The pace was truly frenetic.

Wedding Day

Our wedding day came quickly, yet right on time, sealing our union with a heavenly rubber stamp. The wedding was a time of great joy, celebrating the many answered prayers that brought together two fifty-two-year-old lifelong singles in life-changing fashion. People were genuinely thrilled for us. It was a time to recognize and appreciate what God had done, and to give thanks to those who had stood by us for so many years.

Our wedding assembled the most significant people in our lives. The joy-filled celebration launched us into our tour with great support from family and friends. Our wedding invitation list became the basis for our trip blog reader list. My retirement and Debbie's bridal showers, both at work and with a small church group, also brought significant goodwill to our trip. Because of the novelty of our wedding and trip, the snowballing effect of community and the power of the Internet resulted in total strangers following our journey.

By the time you are fifty-two, you have lived a lot of life and developed a network of friends, associates, and acquaintances that is much bigger than you may realize. Many of these people invested in our trip by showering us with gift cards and cash for equipment purchases or meals along the way. They also would become regular commentators on our trip blog. The warm sentiments, prayers, and shared joy were palpable.

Leaving Maine

With only eleven days between our wedding day and our flight's departure, we had much to accomplish in little time. There had been no doubt in either of our minds that our wedding preparations took precedence over the bike trip preparations. Our goal had been to plan a wedding that would do justice to our union for our own benefit and for the benefit of our loved ones—and we were more than pleased with the results.

Next came the bike tour. And the day of reckoning was upon us. We had merely scraped by with the bare minimum requirements to keep the bike trip dream alive. We wanted a conventional honeymoon apart from the bicycle trip—indeed, our counselors had recommended this hiatus. We also needed to clean out my apartment and say some good-byes.

During a short honeymoon on the Maine coast, we had brought recently acquired bike equipment with us to capitalize on what little training time our tight schedule would allow. We had already made visits and purchases at bicycle shops and recreational outfitters where we had spent considerable time discussing equipment and our impending experience. The advice of these experts and cyclists who had

Organizing bike gear on honeymoon: planned chaos!

already undertaken long-distance bike tours was invaluable. The novelty of our adventure had elicited earnest support on all fronts.

After these consultations, we developed a list of required items, researched the preferred brands, and then acquired the items. It was now time to begin putting the bike trip planning into motion.

Less than two weeks before our intended departure, we had merely accumulated an unorganized pile of stuff, some of which we had no idea how to use. In addition to the typical honeymoon activities, we needed to organize our biking gear, obtain a working knowledge of some of the more technical gear, take a few practice runs on our loaded bikes, and then ship the bicycles west in advance of our arrival. The shipper's lead time was approximately ten days. So, as we continued to bond with one another, we would have little time to bond with our new bicycles before our grand excursion.

In the months leading up to the trip, I was distracted from any reasonable fitness goals because, as I transitioned out of a time- and energy-consuming job, I was simultaneously considering future work options. Furthermore, Debbie and I both lived in the cold New England climate, which limits early season riding. Once warmer weather and longer daylight arrived, we were busy planning both a wedding and a cross-country bicycle trip from scratch! We had virtually no time for serious training.

> As Tim was busy planning for the wedding and the bike trip, I was winding down the school year, which was always a busy time. I was the only literacy specialist in a K-5 elementary school of 600 students, so there was no shortage of work or last-minute requests coming my way. There was simply no time to devote to riding. I was just thankful Tim was not working and could lead the planning for both events. I discovered another one of Tim's gifts: wedding planning!
>
> I had absolutely no idea what it would take to bicycle across the country, but I'd always wanted to. We really didn't talk about whether we could or would "finish." We were more interested in exercising the freedom to embark on this grand adventure as husband and wife.

Debbie and I are health-conscious individuals, but we were far from being in top-notch biking shape. Neither of us typically rode more than 2,000 miles a year. Yet, our planned cross-country route could require as much as 4,000 miles. And we knew we needed to finish before September to accommodate Debbie's return to work. This timetable would no doubt require better fitness than we had after the wedding.

So, at our honeymoon bungalow, we completed our needs list and learned how to pack and ride our new Trek 520 touring bikes. Most touring experts would question the wisdom of venturing into a journey like ours with so little training and riding time. We looked at our trip as diving into the unknown. How our untrained bodies

Abbreviated training with half-loaded bikes atop
Ducktrap Mountain in Northport, Maine

would react to the physical demands was simply another part of the adventure. The trip would be more about the journey than the destination. If we were not able to make it across before Debbie was due to return to school, so what? We'd figure out another way to get home. But in our heart of hearts, it would soon become apparent we were both driven to finish.

After our stay on the Maine coast, it was time to clean out my apartment and put my remaining belongings in storage. I really have never owned much, and I am frugal. Some have described me as a minimalist. But I do have sentimental ties to some things, especially memorabilia. I am learning that personal growth is putting physical possessions in proper perspective. The process of filtering out worthy possessions can be challenging, but also liberating. Some things I'd received as gifts from special people. Other items commemorated special times with those people. Cleaning out the apartment was just another healthy dose of change in a life that had not seen much change. As the ink was still drying on our marriage certificate, perhaps sifting through belongings with Debbie's help was good training for more adjustments ahead! Sleeping on an air mattress was also foreboding. We just hoped our new ones would

Leaving the old single life behind, complete with its trappings!

hold air better than the one we used at the apartment.

As part of our transition and my process of leaving the old life, any belongings we decided to retain were stored in Maine. We did have some negotiations during this weeding-out process. Debbie found little value in most of my possessions—but that was her perspective. She wasn't a sports fan, didn't understand Maine culture, and didn't really know my family. And she wasn't a guy! She also felt as though she already owned all of the amenities we would need as a couple in her fully furnished condominium. She extended sufficient grace to get me through the weeding-out process. Her day of reckoning was yet to come. Long-term, this weeding-out process would be a two-way street, about building a life together, rather than merging the sum of the parts.

So, on the dreary night of June 29, just two days before our plane departed for the West Coast, I left my apartment for good, with my bride alongside. I had no feeling of "good riddance." But neither were there tears—again to my surprise. The only moisture was falling from the heavens. I left the apartment as I had entered it—on a rainy evening. In between fell twenty-five years of life—with its joys, heartaches, relationships, entertainment, work accomplishments, and tears. You can fit a lot of memories into a 600-square-foot apartment! I was ending one of the longest extended-stay motel bookings in history. But tonight wasn't about looking backward. Although I had lived in Maine for fifty of my fifty-two years, I thought, *I could be leaving Bangor and Maine forever.*

I was also leaving a routine, one that had snuck up on me over many years. For five days a week and oftentimes on Saturday, I would wake up, walk a block to work, grab a Subway sandwich for lunch, work late, walk back home to a lifeless dwelling, eat something quick while watching taped news, and go to bed. Toss in a few sporting events and gym workouts for entertainment, and church on Sunday before sleeping off the fog for the rest of the day. Although most facets of this experience were enjoyable, productive, or restorative, the combined routine had become stale. I was thirsty for change. Although I did not know what the future held, I wasn't concerned. I had Debbie and an exciting future. A new day was dawning. I could hardly wait—and I knew Debbie felt the same way.

Winging Our Way West

Our trip to Massachusetts started so late that we booked a room in Portsmouth, New Hampshire, at two in the morning. This presented the first opportunity to address bicycle security. We weren't comfortable leaving our unlocked, rack-mounted bicycles on the car overnight. In what would become a ritual in the days ahead, we wheeled them into our room.

After a late start from the motel the next morning, the first day of July was about to arrive sooner than we wanted. We prepared and packed into the early morning hours. Our turnaround was so demanding that we left many wedding presents unopened. We later discovered that some of them may have come in handy during our trip. While Debbie packed our luggage, I began to set up our new netbook computer. It was one o'clock in the morning. I installed a few essential programs and imported e-mail addresses while we still had access to our other computers and a reliable Internet connection.

Although we had already shipped our bikes west, our bicycling gear would accompany us on the plane. We would fly west with the bare minimum that we would carry on our bicycles. A bargain purchase of two tattered suitcases at the Goodwill store weeks earlier fulfilled a temporary need. We had already purchased panniers. Panniers attach to racks on the bicycle and provide compartments to store gear. I packed them with the belongings we would need for the next two months, distributing the weight in each pannier to accommodate balanced bicycles and to avoid airline baggage fees.

We finally went to bed as daylight began to dawn. A few hours later, we awoke and prepared for our ride to the airport. Chris Brown, a friend, had agreed to give us a ride to the bus stop. When Chris arrived, we were running behind, so she took it upon herself to drive us directly to the airport! This was the first of many acts of kindness we would experience in the next several months.

When Debbie originally contacted her cousin, Jim Massey, to let him know she was getting married and then bicycling across the

Bookended by our pre-trip hosts, Karen and Jim Massey

country, he was excited for us and wanted to help. Jim is a naturopathic doctor who has developed health supplements that he markets through his own business, Mountain Peak Nutritionals. He is also an avid cyclist. Jim and his wife, Karen, live in the Portland, Oregon, area. Jim volunteered to transport us to the Pacific Ocean, simplifying our selection of a route. Some of the best of Adventure Cycling Association's map routes depart from the Astoria, Oregon, area and travel through Portland on their way east along the Columbia River.

When we arrived in Portland, Jim picked us up at the airport and brought us to his home, where we stayed for two nights. Jim and Karen detected our exhaustion and indulged our uninterrupted sleep until eleven o'clock the next morning. Through and through, their support was genuine and generous. Jim took us to several stores to help us stock up on consumables and finish procuring our gear. Jim had also recommended the bike shop to which we had shipped our bicycles. This shop reassembled our bikes and installed some last-minute items, like the handlebar bags and a speedometer for Debbie's bike. They provided great service and shared some trip advice, thanks in part to Jim's familiarity with the staff.

Jim and Tim setting up pannier locking system

Jim and I wrestled with the pannier locking system the night before our departure, which proved to be more challenging than we'd expected. He also gave us a substantial supply of his personally formulated energy drink mix. We would use this mix for several weeks, reminding us daily of his generosity.

Accepting Jim's offer to transport us to the Pacific Ocean allowed us to set up the bikes, complete with loaded panniers, and make adjustments before bicycling on the first day. Once we arrived at our starting point in Seaside, Oregon, we would devote all of our attention to celebrating our departure from the Pacific Ocean, saying our good-byes, and beginning the journey.

Sooner than we knew it, day one of biking arrived. Butterflies leapt within us as Jim helped us load our panniers into his Subaru and attach our bikes to the roof rack. Among our belongings were Adventure Cycling Association maps with our intended turn-by-turn route across America. We'd had no time to study the wealth of trip-planning information on these maps, despite having received them well in advance. Our first serious review of these navigational aids came shortly before departure. Our initial route would take us north

Isabella supervises the loading of gear into the Massey-mobile

along the Oregon coast for sixteen miles. Then we would turn east and head toward the Atlantic.

The anticipation of arriving at the Pacific grew during the hour-long ride. After a seaside photo op, Jim left us with these reminders: "You have a simple repetitive task, which goes as follows: heels down, bring them around! The joy of your journey will not be found in completing it, but in the actual journey itself." Although we agreed with his advice, each of our souls secretly cringed at the thought of not finishing.

> The word "surreal" seems like an oft-overused term. But it aptly describes the emotions that swept over me as I dashed barefoot toward the Pacific surf. I couldn't believe this was happening. Just as the beach sands were powerless to stop the rushing waves, so was I unable to hold my tears. Here I was in the Pacific Northwest for the first time ever—and as a newlywed. The bike trip was at last beginning, triggering the release of emotions accumulated over the preceding weeks. Tears of love, disbelief, awe, and gratitude flooded my cheeks. I had come a long way not only geographically, but also personally and spiritually. I was overwhelmed!

As Debbie enjoyed the setting, I was more focused on the task at hand. I looked at the fully loaded bicycles, not knowing how they would handle or how we would adapt. They never looked or felt so big, so heavy, so awkward. It was "put up or shut up time."

But we also stood before an open book of blank pages, pen in hand—or in front of an artist's empty canvas with palette at the ready. The great escape had happened. We were miles and months away from job responsibilities, financial obligations, past struggles and heartaches, and the daily grind. Despite the impending challenges, the freedom was exhilarating. Life was beginning anew, just as it had weeks earlier when we set sail on the exciting waters of holy matrimony. Yet again, a new day was dawning.

With preparations in hand, Debbie enjoys the Pacific

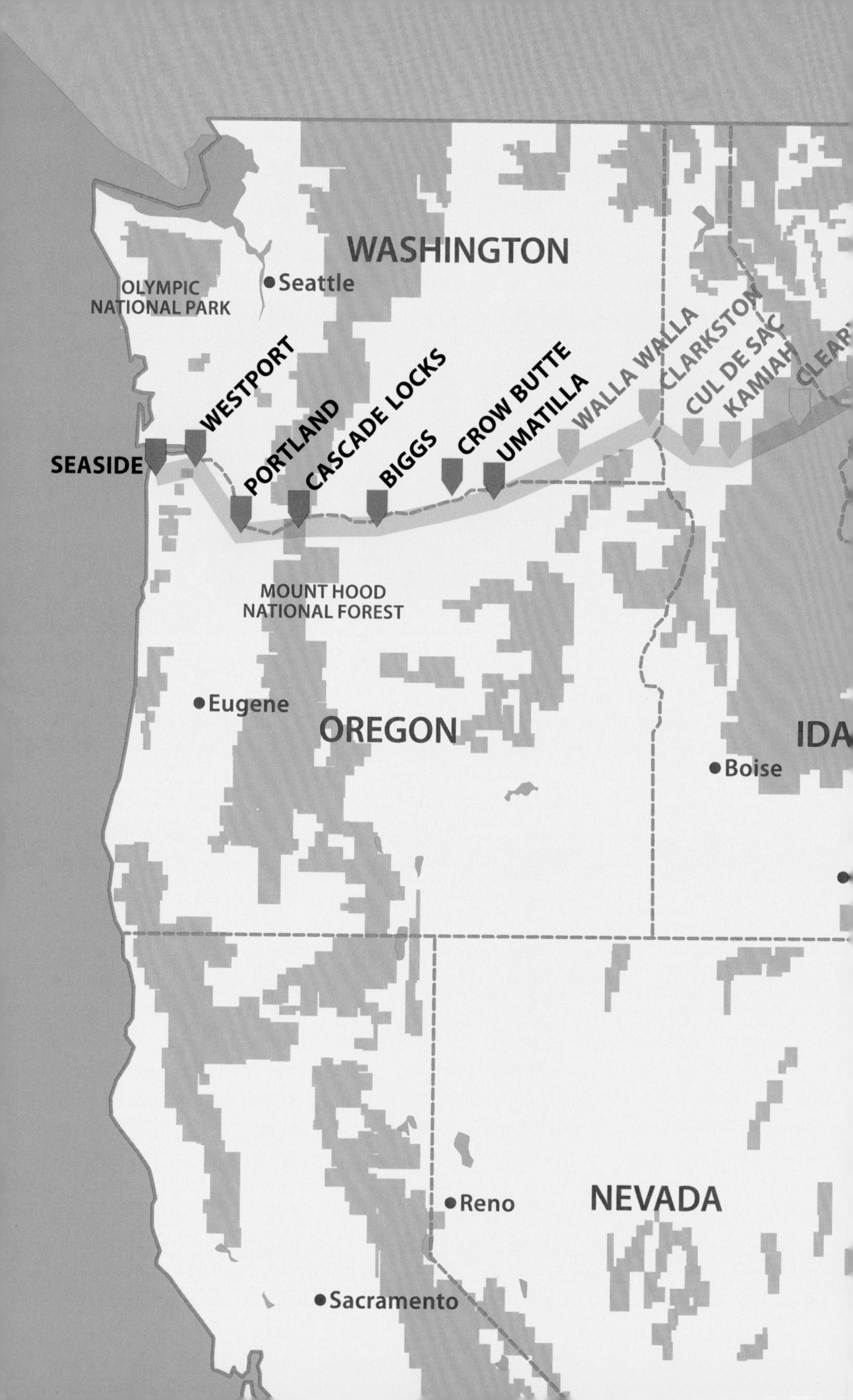
WASHINGTON
OLYMPIC NATIONAL PARK
Seattle
SEASIDE
WESTPORT
PORTLAND
CASCADE LOCKS
BIGGS
CROW BUTTE
UMATILLA
WALLA WALLA
CLARKSTON
CUL DE SAC
KAMIAH
MOUNT HOOD NATIONAL FOREST
Eugene
OREGON
Boise
Reno
NEVADA
Sacramento

4. On-the-Job Training

As Jim's vehicle pulled away, another reality hit home: we were on our own. An interesting assortment of anxiety, adventure, excitement, and satisfaction swept over me. We had a monumental task in front of us. But we had no magical, one-size-fits-all guidebook on how to have a great trip and get home safely. We had chosen to throw that out when we signed up for this trip. Although left to our own devices, we were not alone. We had each other—we were in this together! Accompanied by our modest stash of gear and aids, we could figure this journey out along the way. Debbie and I are both resourceful, task-driven individuals. What better opportunity was there to bond as a team while having the experience of a lifetime? It was a magnificent backdrop to marital bonding, if not bliss—just perfect!

Touring Begins

It was a cloudy day in Seaside, Oregon. This small ocean-side resort town had a summer beach ambiance highlighted by the aqua color of the world's largest ocean. As my wheels began their first turns, I looked down and noticed that the front one was slightly out of true. I had never trued a wheel before. Neither had Debbie. The bike shop where we'd purchased this bicycle had advised me that new bicycle wheels soon fall out of true and would require service well before our journey was completed. Although this minor shimmy was a little sooner than I had expected, I already knew of a good bike shop a hundred miles to the east. The wave of panic soon subsided. I wasn't ready to begin worrying about things I couldn't control. I also wasn't going to make the problem worse by attempting my first repair while we were still in the starting gate.

With our first map displayed clearly through the transparent cover atop my handlebar bag, I plotted the course out of town. We teetered our heavy loads through a few narrow streets and soon came to our first climb. We expected flat terrain along the ocean, so we were surprised at the grade—it wasn't supposed to be like this. We used every low gear on the bike to climb a small, but steep hill, bringing us to a rewarding overlook of the Pacific in the distance. Balancing the awkward load was as much of a challenge as riding the bicycle up the hill. A few negative thoughts immediately tried to steal away the joy of our launch. *I could get off the bike and walk it up the grade,* I thought. And, *If it was this difficult to crawl up a small hill, what will the mountains be like?* However, it was hard to deter our unbridled enthusiasm this early in our trip.

After enjoying the downhill side, Debbie needed to use the bathroom several miles later. We hadn't really given much thought to bathroom breaks. We assumed there would be plenty of facilities along the way. However, bicycle travel occurs at a much slower pace than automobile travel. There are not convenient facility stops every ten miles. Neither was the map route designed with "nature breaks" in mind.

> When we were married and decided to go on this bike trip, it hadn't occurred to me I would need to expose myself to my husband out in the wild. I just assumed we could find restrooms along the way. Boy, was I wrong! My fantasy of being an irresistible wife was shattered when we hunted for the first "open air" restroom. I processed so much fluid while pedaling that frequent and urgent stops became the norm. It was initially uncomfortable for both of us. But, in time, Tim became my scout and watch guard, making sure I wasn't exposing myself to anyone and everyone. These inconvenient and awkward moments were a small price to pay for the journey ahead.

We soon brought our marital bonding to a more intimate level with impromptu rest stops along the side of the road. Thankfully, at least on this day, we had cover. A packet of moist towelettes and a ziplock plastic bag soon became useful accoutrements in Debbie's handlebar bag.

We had departed Seaside around noontime. We soon made it to Astoria and turned the corner to head east along the Columbia River. Riding was slow. I began to consider where we would stay for the evening. Sure, we'd brought a tent and sleeping bags, so what was the worry? But upon further reflection, one can't just set up camp anywhere. This was another assumption gone bad. We began to pay closer attention to the map for towns that might have accommodations. By early evening, I was getting antsy. Despite the relatively short mileage, we needed a place to stay.

We rolled into Westport and immediately spotted an older-looking motel that no doubt had hosted many a cross-country cyclist in its day. Much to our relief, they had a vacant room. The proprietor said the room was small, but it would fit our bicycles. When I asked about whether the motel offered Wi-Fi Internet access, she said they had paid for it but couldn't get it to work. I agreed to look at it to see if I could help. It was purely from selfish motives because we hadn't posted any blog entries yet. In fact, we weren't really sure how, and we had people interested in knowing where we were and whether we were safe.

We checked in and cleaned up. We had bicycled forty-seven miles. It was a good day for starters. I told Debbie that if we were to bicycle 4,000 miles across the country, and if we averaged only fifty miles a day, it would take eighty days without any rest days. We had less than sixty days. We would need to average at least seventy-five miles a day—and we were already twenty-eight miles behind that pace. It would be interesting to see what pace we would develop in the first week to support our dream of reaching the Atlantic.

Our room was on the east side of the building, where we were happy to see an adjacent community church. The next day was Sunday. We could visit the church in the morning before we left town. Church is important to us. We don't attend church out of obligation, and we don't think God has a point system for attendance. But it does encourage us. We find we can share meaningfully with others who believe in God. We may have something to offer them and they may have something to offer us. But if we don't come together at church, we will miss that sharing opportunity.

After changing, we walked across the street to a conveniently located restaurant. A poodle named Troll, along with its owner, seated us. Our twenty-year-old waitress was friendly, but seemed in need of some guidance. She was the first person on our trip with whom we shared TheHopeLine.

We had chosen to promote TheHopeLine (thehopeline.com) on our trip as a way of expressing our appreciation to God and to give something back. TheHopeLine is a help service that seeks to reach and rescue hurting teens and young adults. Trained Hope Coaches handle toll-free phone calls and Internet chats from youth in crisis and seek to listen, encourage, apply Scripture, and pray for their issues. Hope Coaches will refer these youth to partner agencies that offer expertise with issues such as suicide, addiction, and abuse.

Donning T-shirts we printed to promote TheHopeLine

Debbie and I are both volunteer Hope Coaches.

Our primary tool to promote TheHopeLine would be one-on-one contact with potential donors, volunteers, and troubled youth. The organization had sent us promotional cards to distribute. There were two types: one designed to help recruit more coaches and raise support; another to inform youth of the toll-free phone number and website address. Our waitress received the smaller youth card. We later prayed she would call the number.

After supper, we returned to the motel. With the flurry of pre-trip activities since our wedding, and after spending the past two nights with the Masseys, it had been awhile since Debbie and I had any flexibility over our short-term priorities. Debbie worked on the blog for a short time while I reviewed the map. Since the only consistent Internet access was at the motel office, we wouldn't be spending much time on the computer tonight. That was just as well. It had been only two weeks since our wedding night. Our tiny room became a cozy room leading to the first of many memorable motel stays on our trip. We like being married!

Independence Day

Navigating over our first threshold in Westport, Oregon

At church the next morning, July 4, and for many of the Sundays during our trip, we talked to the pastor after the service and gave him some of TheHopeLine cards. We also began a process of dropping a recruiting card at most of the churches we passed. We would plant the youth cards where youth might find them. And many a young waitress would find one nestled under her tip money.

As with the first day, the weather and scenery as we rode toward Portland were unspectacular. One uncertainty going into our trip was how we would handle the hills with our heavy loads and new bicycles. Our first serious test came as we approached a steep grade on busy US Route 30. There was no shoulder, merely a slow traffic lane—slow traffic in name only. Without a shoulder, we would need to share space with fast-moving vehicles approaching from behind as we ambled up the hill. We struggled to balance our bulky, awkward loads. Because this was day two and we had not trained with a comparable load, and now burdened with what we later learned was an excessive amount of food, we wobbled up the long, steep hill. We began to wonder how we would fare when we hit the real mountains, the Rockies!

Partway up the hill, which rose 800 feet in three miles, was a dirt driveway forking off at a 45-degree angle. We decided to roll off the pavement onto the driveway to allow traffic to clear and to catch our breath. When we attempted to resume our climb, we were unable to balance and start our bicycles from a dead stop. This was our first lesson in hill climbing: never stop when climbing a steep grade! Rather than admit defeat and walk our bicycles up the remainder of the hill, whose end was not in sight, we decided to coast the bikes back down the grade, using the dirt driveway as a launching pad. Once we had achieved enough speed to balance the bikes, we would turn back uphill. The challenge of this approach was to proceed only when there was an ample break in the traffic on this busy road. We would need to turn the bicycles 135 degrees to head up the hill. Herein lay another lesson: these loaded bikes could not turn on a dime. In fact, they could barely turn in the three lanes of roadway we had here! After waiting for the opportune time, we conquered the remainder of the hill.

Our lunch stop came at a very familiar site—a Subway restaurant. Right beside the Subway was a Starbucks. We spotlighted these two franchises at our wedding reception. I earned a reputation over many years as one of Subway's most loyal customers. I was a three- or four-day-a-week lunch patron of a nearby shop within short walking distance from work. The staff there was so familiar with me and my preferences that they would begin making my sandwich the minute I came through the door, with no instructions required. And although I don't drink coffee, Debbie does—in potent dosages. Starbucks is her favorite brand. Familiarity sometimes breeds comfort, so for a short time, we dipped back into our former lives in this distant land. Enjoying a "footlong" and refreshing drinks energized us for our evening ride.

Familiarity breeds comfort

On the way to Portland, a ramshackle pickup truck stopped just ahead of us. A scraggly man emerged from the cab and asked if we would like to stay at his place, just around the corner, for the evening.

I was thankful Tim turned him down without any serious consideration. From all appearances, he may have been out to gag us, tie us to chairs, and sell our bicycles and equipment on the Internet. I had heard about cross-country cyclists receiving such offers, but hadn't really considered what those offers might look or feel like—until now.

First up was the magnificent St. John's Bridge, a Gothic-style suspension bridge spanning the Willamette River. We arrived after suppertime to sparse traffic. The bridge crossing offered beautiful vistas. From the center deck, the lateral sun shone unblocked from downstream, shimmering on the water's surface in either direction before slipping away moments later. We rode through seemingly endless neighborhoods. People milled around on side streets in anticipation of twilight fireworks. Wow! I would never have guessed Portland, Oregon, was so large. But then again, I'd never been to Portland, Oregon.

St. John's Bridge, Portland, Oregon

Meanwhile, Debbie was feeling that urge again to go to the bathroom. Despite the population density, there seemed to be no services along our residential route. Even I felt the pressure from her bladder as it again dawned on me that my bride needed a place to stay this evening. Eventually, we found a mission on a street corner that reluctantly let Debbie use their bathroom. I guess I can't blame them because we interrupted their video. They were more interested in the storyline within than in engaging two travelers in search of services.

As our ride resumed, I continued to lead us along the map route. What else did I know? I was beginning to wonder whether I had a false confidence that we would soon hit the city limits, a highway interchange, or a random spot where motel lodging and restaurants would emerge, bringing our prolonged ride into the dusk to a restful end. When a detour forced us off the map route, yesterday's panicky feeling returned. However, as if by providence, our detoured route immediately led us to an Econo Lodge with a McDonald's and a few convenience stores on abutting corners of a major intersection. With much to celebrate in our own lives, this would be our perch for a multi-directional fireworks display to celebrate our nation's birth. The spray of colors and the crackling and popping of explosives provided enjoyment and comfort after the long ride.

Our arrival at the motel triggered an urge to work on the blog. We were slipping behind in our desire to let others know how we were doing. Like our pace for riding, ground lost on one day would need to be made up on another. We were just acclimating to life on the road and life with each other. A delicate balancing act of making progress on multiple fronts was an instructional tutorial on married life. Among the competing interests was the need for some rest. Seventy-two miles, thanks to the late northwestern sunset, may have been short of our goal once again, but it still took significant time and energy. Our untrained bodies were understandably tired. So, we bid a late evening "Happy birthday" to America and a "Good night" from Portland, Oregon.

There is only one original!

The Gorgeous Gorge

Our third day on the road would bring us to high and lofty places. A spectacular diversity of landscapes awaited our escape from city limits. Our departure seemed endless due to Portland's large footprint. Debbie and I enjoyed interesting stops and beautiful scenery on our first day along the Columbia River Gorge. We climbed to a high overlook east of Portland, from which the gorge appeared in splendid beauty. When we arrived at Chanticleer Point, the artists were busy with futile attempts to replicate the Master Artist's touch.

Visible from this lofty perch was Crown Point, a lookout in its own right, featuring a rotunda providing beautiful views in multiple directions. As we made our way from Chanticleer Point to Crown Point and beyond along the Old Columbia River Highway, we rode under forest canopies while seeing and hearing several grand waterfalls flowing from high above. At the bottom of this descent was the impressive Multnomah Falls, a magnificent falls that attracts many tourists. The old scenic highway continues along the Columbia River at sufficient altitude to provide beautiful overlooks, high above the speedy traffic on Interstate 84 that runs adjacent to the river and accompanying rail line. We passed through an intriguing set of tunnels and followed the old road, which often felt more like a trail than a highway. As we traversed this gorgeous stretch of landscape, we stopped for frequent photo ops or to fathom the abundant beauty. *This is the stuff honeymoons are made of,* I thought.

Multnomah Falls

Top: Columbia River Gorge from Chanticleer Point
Bottom: Views of the Columbia River with Interstate 84 alongside

In the back of my head, though, there was the constant ticktock as more miles stole away from our daily average. We could choose to travel slowly, engage more people, and see more sights. Or we could choose to keep a faster pace that would allow us to sightsee, but also enable us to cycle coast to coast. My penchant for work, productivity, and achieving goals suggested the latter option would offer more long-lasting satisfaction. Speeding up the pace also needed to mesh with our on-the-job training for bicycle touring. Although our minds may have wanted to push the pace, our bodies and emotions were not ready. Neither were our raw rear ends.

One such example of fatigue occurred on an isolated country road in the Columbia River valley. Early in the day, we encountered a small hill with a steep grade. There was no sign on the grade, but it must have been at least 12 percent.

As I ascended the grade, I ever so slowly crisscrossed the entire road, first from right to left, and then back again, to reduce the climb's pitch. It was a very short hill—I could see the top just ahead. But it was so steep that my leg strength gave out as I struggled to propel the heavy bike. Suddenly, I lost it. The bicycle toppled, with me on it. Frustrated, I began again, side to side, inching along. But again, I fell—and I cried. *How am I going to do this?* I thought. *Surely, there will be steeper climbs in the mountains.* This was beginning to feel too much like work and not enough like fun. Tim, true to his nature, just continued along, seemingly insensitive to what was happening inside of me.

I didn't exactly power my bicycle up this hill, but Debbie's trouble on the hill really made me wonder how we would do later. I knew she was very determined on physical endeavors, so I assumed she would use challenges as motivation. I really thought she was carrying proportionately too much weight for her size, but I would let her come to that realization on her own. Consistent with her work ethic, she wanted to carry her own load, both figuratively and literally.

Another incident in the gorge demonstrated just how hazardous the road could be. We were cycling on Interstate 84, where the roar of the truck traffic made communication virtually impossible. Interstate cycling is prohibited in most places, but not here. And according to our map, this was the optimal route on this leg of our journey. Debbie had a near brush with death. Riding behind her at the time, I saw it unfold before my very eyes.

Interstate biking in the shadow of Mount Hood

I was approaching a slow-moving maintenance vehicle on the shoulder. To the left of the vehicle, separating the shoulder from the travel lane, was a deep rumble strip. Undeterred and daydreaming, I swung to the left, slowly passing the vehicle. All of a sudden, a precariously close, fast-moving tractor trailer started to whiz by on my left. My heart began to race. When my front wheel struck one of the ruts in the rumble strip, the fork swiveled out of control, jeopardizing the balance of the bike. Although the tractor trailer was making a very cozy, high-speed pass, I thought it would never clear me. The loud roar alongside was frightening and I was losing control of the bike. But somehow, I saved it.

I love to downhill ski—the closer to the edge, the more thrilling the run. But I have to admit, dancing side by side with an eighteen-wheeler gave me a new appreciation for the hazards of the road. I like my life—there is too much to live for, especially now. The incident caused me to think and consider *What if...?* I became more aware of safety on the remainder of the trip. I decided to try a rearview mirror. And now I would never do another bicycle ride without one.

My suspicion is adrenaline assisted in Debbie's Houdini act. I was amazed she was able to prevent the bike from crashing. It took superhuman reflexes and strength to right her slowly moving, unbalanced bicycle and to power it out of the rumble strip. To this day, I still can't believe she saved it. Debbie enjoys extreme thrills, but this one must have been too much for even her.

After my own adrenaline rush passed, we soon left the highway to safer places. When I consider what could have happened, it is a horrific memory. Here I was, a newlywed, realizing I could have lost the woman I had waited all my life to marry. I could only thank God that He had spared my wife. There was comfort in knowing He was watching out for us.

There are lessons in a narrow escape like this. The first is to recognize that potential catastrophes lurk, not only for a cross-country cyclist, but also for everyone. On our trip, our vulnerability added significantly to the adventure and, therefore, the satisfaction of the tour. Facing challenging circumstances beckons resourcefulness and faith, which often leads to personal growth. Overcoming challenges reinforces your confidence in both your ability to cope and the object of your faith. If you dwell too much on potential problems, you will never make it out of your driveway! Although it took courage to move forward, we weren't about to let fear and intimidation keep us from realizing our dream. To succumb would have been to surrender freedom and become shackled to our fears.

The Desert Awaits

The hilly bicycling terrain of Oregon, even in the Columbia River Gorge, surprised us. Cycling close to a river, one would assume flat terrain, but for the past few days, this clearly had not been the case. The Columbia River separates the states of Oregon and Washington. A few nights ago, we had walked a bridge over the Columbia after dark just to claim entry into Washington. On this day, we would spend most of our time there.

Another surprise came on our fifth day of bicycling. The cool temperatures in the 60s of the past several days had begun to change. Now we would ride in near 100-degree heat in the middle of a desert! How could this happen in one of the northernmost states in our nation? After four days on the road, we still felt uncertainty about how we would fare for the entire journey. We were tired, our bodies and behinds were tattered, and our mileage was modest. We continued to struggle with riding, our schedule, catching up on the blog, and, at times, one another.

Desert travel in Washington state

Mount Hood disappearing in the rearview mirror

We left the trucker's junction at Biggs, Oregon, after a good night's sleep, crossing the Columbia River into Washington and connecting to Route 14, the Lewis and Clark Highway. Adventure Cycling Association's maps, in fact, referred to the first half of our entire planned route as the Lewis and Clark Trail. Their maps follow roughly the same journey, from St. Louis to Astoria, of the famous explorers of the nineteenth century. We would follow this route into Montana, and then join the so-called Northern Tier route.

Ten miles into our ride, our first encounter with dogs was about to happen. I really don't like hearing a dog bark when I'm bicycling. And I like it even less when I can see them running at me. When I hear their excited barks and ominous growls, adrenaline begins to kick in. When I see their curled lips, sharp teeth, and the cold look in their eyes, chills travel the full length of my spine.

There they were: three big ones. I could see them from afar as they began barking and sprinting down their owner's driveway, launched like a triad of missiles at the prospect of fresh meat. The driveway was about the size of a football field, so I had some time to gather my thoughts. They seemed on pace to intercept me when I arrived at the end of what had become their racetrack. And Debbie was several feet behind me. Surely, no one on this isolated stretch of road would be investing in invisible fence technology, but I could hold out hope. Since Debbie had our only can of pepper spray, it would do me little good. And another troubling thought occurred to me: *If I get through this pack in one piece, what about Debbie? She's lagging behind and sure to encounter these snarling canines.* Nevertheless, I wasn't inclined to stop and serve up lunch on a silver platter to these mutts.

When the three dogs reached the end of the long drive-way and swarmed Tim's bike, I had a front row seat to the horror show. I reached for the can of pepper spray as the first and most aggressive dog lunged at Tim, circled his bike, and clenched his teeth onto something on the right side of Tim's bike. Tim just kept on riding, dragging the dog for several feet until it let go. At first, I couldn't tell whether the muscle dog had sunk his teeth into Tim's leg. But it was his pannier instead. I couldn't believe how calm Tim was. Thankfully, a passing vehicle with heavenly timing herded the troublemaking hounds and sent them on their way home. We escaped unscathed despite our heightened pulses.

Many dogs have chased me over my years of bicycling, but never multiple dogs at the same time. After our frightful encounter early in the day, I thought about how defenseless we were on these bicycles. Pepper spray is a logical defense, but it needs to be readily available. Even if I'd had the spray in my bag, opening it while riding would have been tricky. After all, I was using both hands to balance the bicycle. And even if I'd had it in my hand, I would have needed a good aim to make a difference. Another school of thought is to spray water in the dog's face. However, even if I could have squirted it effectively with one hand, water was becoming a valuable commodity on this very hot day. I also wondered what might have happened if these dogs had gotten in front of me while I was traveling at high speed. Crashing could have been the worst result. As in life, unforeseen pitfalls lurk. But you can't let that stop you from running the race.

Even without the dog attack, Route 14 proved to be an intimidating stretch of road. What initially seemed like pleasurable warmth on a wide-open, well-paved, and well-shouldered road became a most discouraging and seemingly endless journey to nowhere in oppressive heat. To make matters worse, a persistent headwind whistled into our helmets. Without the anticipated prevailing westerly wind, it felt as though we were biking uphill. The more energy we expended, the stronger the wind, or so it seemed. Before we knew it, we were in a desert, and we were parched.

The surroundings were plain—and redundant. There were no services for miles—only brown rolling hills covered with windmills to our left, oversized tractor trailers speeding by with their toxic cargo headed to a remote landfill, sagebrush along the roadside, and an adjacent rail line separating us from the deep blue Columbia River to our right. The only redeeming features were the strong aroma of sage and the beauty of the clear, deep blue sky, which joined the Columbia River in providing rich color to an otherwise bland environment. Occasionally, the tires of a passing vehicle would strike the center-of-road rumble strip, creating a startling, intimidating noise that prevented any idle thoughts.

After thirty-five blisteringly hot miles into the headwind, a small village appeared, an oasis in the desert. On a stretch of road like this, you can't be too choosy about where you stop, especially in the heat. So, we hitched our bicycles beside a pickup truck and entered a windowless saloon, nervously leaving all of our possessions out of our sight. The saloon provided shade, lunch, and plenty of cold energy drinks. The locals told us about a campground, formerly run by the state, twenty-odd miles up the road. Given our current speed, we would not make it to a motel for the evening. But it was comforting that we now had a goal.

Before resuming our ride, we simultaneously visited the saloon's respective his and hers restrooms, each wallpapered with life-sized pinups of naked models of the opposite sex. Back at the bar, we traded notes to confirm that we had indeed arrived in the Wild West, or at least a modern-day version of it. We quickly came to appreciate that our chosen method of travel and unfamiliarity with our surroundings would subject us to a wide variety of settings, some of which we would not otherwise choose. Nevertheless, we had received what we needed: rest, a cool-down, a delicious meal, and local advice. And we were more than ready to move on.

Around eight o'clock, we approached the campground at Crow Butte, Washington. Our desert environs immediately blossomed into lush greenery. The campground was set on an island in the Columbia River, adjoining the mainland with a causeway. The causeway became our first setting for a bicycle repair. Debbie's front tire had gone flat after striking a blunt crevice in the road entering the park. We took some comfort in knowing that our accommodations lay just around the corner. But it would soon be dark, so a quick repair job was in our best interests. We still needed to eat supper, and who knew how that would come together?

When you sustain a flat tire in the wild, you soon remember your limitations. Neither Debbie nor I am mechanically inclined. We were carrying only two spare tubes. Given the long distance between services on this stretch of road, my first concern was fixing the flat without wasting either of them. Who knew where we would find the next store that carried spare tubes? So, I decided to put a patch on the tube in order to maximize our repair stash, even though I had never successfully patched a leaking tube. My customary practice would have been to replace the tube.

I repaired the tube and all seemed well. We pulled up to an empty gatehouse, which was closed for the evening, and then rode into the park. A campground worker and his friendly little mascot dog, the copilot of his golf cart, met us on the road into the campground. We checked in and proceeded to the tenting area. A conspicuous sign warning of rattlesnakes suggested we pitch our tent near the center of the complex. It also acted as a reminder of our vulnerability. From the center of the campground, we would benefit from a short walk to the bathroom with, hopefully, no snake bites. There could be no guarantee about our fellow campers, of course. Sometimes, the wildest creatures of all are those who walk around on two feet. But we couldn't worry about that now.

Let's pitch our tent elsewhere!

Infighting

Our first night of camping revealed just how inexperienced we were. It took a long time to set up camp and prepare the evening's meal. We awoke the next morning to find Debbie's front tire flat once again. The patch had failed. I was determined to use the patch kit to fix the second flat, even though Debbie wanted me to use a tube. Although she had already voiced the reasonable expectation that we leave earlier in the morning to maximize the daylight, cooler temperatures, and our own energy levels, I felt that we needed to know how to patch blown tubes.

> I could have wrapped that blown tube around his neck! We were stuck at the campground until one thirty in the afternoon while he refused to slap a spare tube in the tire. He ended up doing this anyway when the patch job failed a second time. We were just wasting valuable time while the heat was getting more and more intense.

Going into the trip, we were both oblivious about the requirements and time demands of a cross-country bicycle tour. We thought we would have plenty of time to knock out the miles and immerse ourselves in one another. We did not appreciate the difficulty of communicating with any depth while riding. In short, like marriage, the beginner goes into a trip like this with certain expectations that may or may not be realistic. When reality hits, adjustments are necessary. Our life experience and maturity would help us adapt, but it wasn't easy. We would need to assess what was important and let go of the rest, saving our energy for better things.

Once back out in the desert, the temperatures were again extreme, into the mid-90s. My relentlessness on the repair job produced a heat index between the two of us that rivaled the ambient temperature.

> I wanted to stop for a swim in the river. Although Tim may have had a point about the hazards of navigating across the railroad tracks and through the brush to get to the river, he

was just no fun to be around—at least not on this day. I quietly considered flying home from the next airport. I questioned whether it was worth continuing.

Debbie hadn't drawn the connection between dead snake skins on the highway, the "Beware of Rattlesnakes" sign at the campground, and tall brush near a river. With enough negative vibes to send us off in opposite directions, we shortened the day early, arriving in Umatilla, Oregon, and checking into a motel.

We had been in close quarters for over a week now and tensions were high. Debbie cooled off in the pool while I worked on the blog. A brief online video chat with Mom later that evening helped to alleviate some of the tension. Our daily commitment to read the Bible and pray before bed would help more, as would a good night's sleep. But, with the discord, our morale was ebbing. We had much self-doubt regarding our will and ability to complete our journey. Thirty-seven miles was not going to advance us toward our goals. But neither was the strife between us.

It reminded me of a conversation in the bike shop before we embarked. The employees who helped outfit our trip said it would be a miracle if we were still married when we returned. They knew something about the close quarters, intense experience, and unique stresses of a cross-country bike ride, as well as a new marriage, that we did not fully appreciate—until now. This trip would either help bond us together or put a wedge between us. Conventional wisdom says that the best way to learn a language is by total immersion. At this point in the journey, we had reached total marriage immersion. Because we came together later in life, we had some lost time to make up for; we wanted to quickly create a meaningful life together, as one. We were determined to

use the bike trip to help expedite our bonding. After all, none of us knows when he or she will breathe in his or her last breath. The bike trip could help maximize our sacred union by kick-starting us into living our remaining days to the full. But it was now time to merely right the ship.

> I thought the bike trip was going to be all about us. I later came to realize there was more to it than that. Yes, there was the pleasure of being alone with Tim and discovering what he was all about. But there were also daily tasks and hard work upon which our success depended. We had the privilege of telling others about TheHopeLine. And we chose to share our experience with others on the blog. While I first saw the blog as an unnecessary time-waster, I am now grateful we invested the couple of hours a day needed to document and share our adventure.

Pre-marital counseling helps a couple identify some of their stronger compatibilities as well as those areas where they may struggle. The results of our counseling suggested we would be very good at conflict resolution. We now needed these skills on a regular basis. In making their tongue-in-cheek assessment, the bike shop helpers were not privy to our shared passion for athletic challenges and bicycling, Debbie's adventuresome spirit, and our shared faith in God. They also did not realize we are strong bikers when we are in good riding shape. Although we were inexperienced with bicycle touring and marriage, we were both determined enough to convert an inference we could not do something into a challenge to help motivate us toward success.

Debbie and I are quite different when it comes to adventure, planning, and due diligence. I am an accountant and business-man by trade. In my last job, being aware of and managing risks was paramount. I have also played a great deal of competitive chess, where one little slip-up can be catastrophic. I have learned over the years to consider carefully the consequences of important decisions. Debbie, on the other hand, is a classic thrill-seeker. She believes in quick, intuitive decisions and likes to sample diverse experiences. As a teacher, she relishes learning by experience. Isn't it interesting that God has brought together two people with these different profiles? By design, a built-in tension pushes both of us toward middle ground.

As it did coming into Umatilla, this tension played out dramatically on the remainder of our bike trip. There were cautions on my radar, specifically when we were moving into depressed areas with higher crime tendencies or when violent weather was in the forecast. Debbie's method of dealing with these risks would be to proceed and react, whereas I would gather more information and try to understand the alternatives better before proceeding. We addressed each situation on its own merits.

Together, we would need to meet somewhere in between. Such is the essence of two being better than one. We are pulled out of our own bastion of comfort, sometimes willingly, sometimes kicking and screaming, and learn there are other viewpoints, methods, and approaches. Self-interest no longer rules—or it shouldn't—for there is a collective interest now. Our own little world becomes a bit bigger, with broader vision, but also with deeper personal enrichment. Unless you plan to travel through life alone, you, too, will encounter these interpersonal dynamics.

Today, we are able to joke about Umatilla, Oregon, a testing ground for our trip and our relationship. In life, it pays to choose your travel partner wisely. Just two days after our meltdown, we would enjoy one of the more delightful and rewarding days of the entire trip.

Where to now?

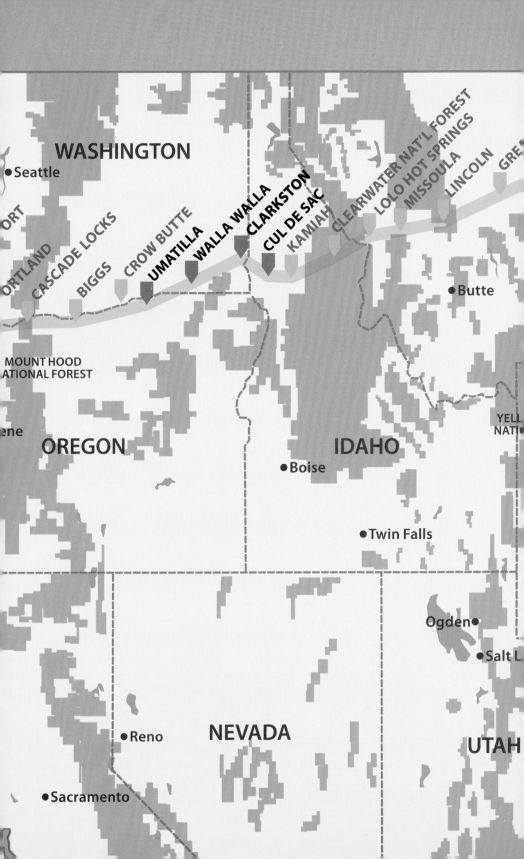

5. Climbing Out of the Valley

THE SUN AROSE AGAIN ON THE NEXT MORNING. We were soon off to Walla Walla, Washington, choosing to leave the figurative black cloud of Umatilla behind us. This new day would present its own unique challenges. The temperature was well into the 90s again. We traveled fifty-four miles and reached our destination. A convenience store on the outskirts of town offered a surprisingly healthy menu for lunch. It was also a satisfactory albeit makeshift rest stop to catch up on phone calls. These were not just any phone calls. While I was providing feedback to the lead director of the board for the company I had just left, Debbie's conversation was even weightier.

Revisiting Life's Problems

Before our trip, the company's president had requested I participate in an exit interview with the lead director of the board. The lead director and I had swapped messages, but been unable to connect. Because two months had passed since my departure from the company, I considered this interview to be a mere formality. Nevertheless, it seemed right to respond—right for the betterment of a company I had helped advance for years and right for the benefit of the many friends left behind to carry on. Somehow, revisiting prior work relationships, business challenges, and frustrations; providing honest and balanced assessments on leadership; and stepping back into a world I had chosen to leave behind seemed to fly in the face of the purpose and spirit of our cross-country bicycle excursion. Yet, I responded to the questions as openly and honestly as I could, entrusting the board to handle the feedback appropriately. Deep within, I was disappointed they had not sought my opinion earlier, but at least this was an opportunity to offer constructive criticism, while resisting the urge to grind any axe.

I returned a call to my sister Ayme while Tim was following up with his former employer. In order to preserve our pristine honeymoon, Ayme had chosen not to tell me about Dad's most recent health issue. He had fallen at the airport when returning from our wedding. He had sustained some head trauma and was experiencing mini strokes. His health was failing. When she handed the phone to him, I couldn't control my emotions any longer. His slurred and confused speech sounded so sad that it broke my heart to listen. Just three weeks earlier, he was walking me down the aisle.

During my lengthy call, I noticed Debbie was crying on her phone call. Her conversation with her father was brief, but tearful. It summoned a question we had considered several weeks ago. What would we do if one of our elderly parents became ill or passed away during our trip? We had agreed this possibility—or probability, given the age and health of our parents—should not stop us from embarking. If you worry about what might happen, you will have great difficulty accomplishing, let alone pursuing, any goals and dreams. We would need to deal with such circumstances as they arose. This was our first case in point.

After talking with her sister, Debbie had virtually resolved this question before we even spoke. Although it was difficult to assess without being there, her dad's condition did not appear acute nor life threatening. We would continue on, comforted in knowing we had shared meaningfully with him at our wedding. Our life was just blossoming while his could be fading. It seemed appropriate that our life go on uninterrupted, at least until the next phone call from home.

Retooling

After several days away from any towns offering bicycle repair services, our search for a bicycle shop had been a primary consideration of our ride into town. We needed to stock up on spare tubes and address saddle sores. Another day of relatively low mileage seemed less important than improving the quality of our riding, discovering our surroundings, and enjoying one another. We had plenty of time to arrange for transportation home, whatever that might entail.

When we spotted a shop shortly before closing, we felt like we had discovered water in the middle of a desert. I wasn't going to skimp on tubes this time. I also purchased some cream for sore bums. Each of us purchased a pair of bicycling shorts. The counsel we received from the shop owner proved as valuable as the merchandise we purchased. Quality shorts that fit well and minimized stitching in awkward places would make a big difference for us. We had no suspicion of hearing another sales pitch on expensive equipment from a bicycle shop. We were eager to try any promising solution. The proprietor also reinforced the importance of cleansing, prompting a trip to the grocery store thereafter for some alcohol swabs.

"Alcohol swabs?" one might ask. We intended to use them to eliminate bacteria in the groin area, which should translate to fewer sores. We had received conflicting advice about alcohol swabs before the trip began. But based upon how our bottoms were feeling, we didn't care about any stinging. We wanted to use the best option available to address this issue before it got out of control, if it wasn't already. So, we began treating one another after cycling each day with a gentleness and a compassion we did not realize was within us. This wasn't the type of intimacy we longed for before getting married. But, as a married couple, we realized that everything we have and are belongs to one another. When that first swab hit my raw bottom, believe me, it did sting. It reminded me of when Mom used to treat an open wound with iodine or isopropyl alcohol, but it felt much worse because of the area's tenderness. I think Debbie thought my flinching and yelping were overreactions, but it hurt that badly.

Having extra time on another shortened day allowed us to enjoy the sights and sounds of Walla Walla, a quaint, isolated town with character. A small musical ensemble from North Carolina was in the center of town entertaining a leisure gathering. Alluring aromas in the bakery and candy shops prompted us to settle in for supper across the street at the pizza joint. We had ample time to rest and do laundry in a commercial washer and dryer. I also swapped out my bicycle seat to see if that would help alleviate the saddle sores. Because I had been unable to assess seats before embarking, I had brought my road bike seat as a spare. Given how much I was suffering, I had nothing to lose by trying another seat.

A Day to Remember

With the desert surroundings of the past several days, we had little expectations for beautiful scenery until we encountered the Rocky Mountains. On our eighth day of riding, however, we rolled out of Walla Walla and into a surprisingly delightful world filled with breathtaking landscapes, tranquility, and some long, gradual, exhilarating descents. The beauty and serenity of the lush golden wheat fields of the Middle Waitsburg Road overwhelmed us as they ushered us through the rolling hills to new heights. Red poppies swayed along a fence that encircled only one of many wheat fields ripe for the harvest. The curvy ascent along this memorable stretch paved the way for a breathtaking downhill ride amid wheat and windmills.

> What beauty and peacefulness! The tranquility was in stark contrast to the oppressive heat and strife of the prior days. Although the temperature was still in the 90s, some cloud cover, a gentle tailing breeze, and virtually no traffic made for ideal riding conditions. What a difference when the wind fills your sail from behind rather than head-on. Even the name of the town, Waitsburg, fit our story well. Our loads floated as our souls ingested this glorious breath of fresh air. The last few days were like boot camp. But this day was like a combat soldier receiving a letter from home—a heaven-sent reminder of one's purpose.

Beautiful wheat fields in eastern Washington

A tranquil and serene setting

We met a busload of youth and their chaperones in Dayton, Washington, where we stopped for lunch. They were returning from a weeklong church camp trip in Montana. We engaged some of the adults and shared TheHopeLine with them. When we mentioned the name of the "face" of the organization, one of the chaperones—a missionary on leave from Mexico—exclaimed, "Dawson McAllister? He's the youth pastor for America!" TheHopeLine flyer intrigued him. He wondered whether he could coach in another country. Perhaps it was something in the air, but the people with whom we spoke on this day were particularly friendly, interested, and supportive. Their encouragement was energizing.

We enjoyed three pleasurable descents. The first was about 500 feet; the second, 1,100 feet; and the last, 1,900 feet. How amazing to coast, apply brakes, and still carry thirty-eight miles per hour down the road. I hit forty-one miles per hour on one of the steeper descents. The king of the three descents occurred near the seventy-five-mile mark after a gradual climb to Alpowa Summit.

Sun sets on hills by the Snake River

The ride down the other side covered twelve miles, dropping nearly 2,000 feet of elevation on a smooth, well-shouldered, and sparsely traveled road. The grade was perfect—little braking was needed and periodic bursts of pedaling merely added to the fun, enhancing the coasting and hastening the day's trip. The eastern decline from Alpowa Summit set a high standard for future joyrides.

We rolled into Clarkston, Washington, on the banks of the Snake River and the Idaho border. Clarkston bears the name of one of the early explorers whose trail we were following. A sister city, Lewiston, across the Snake River in Idaho, bears the name of Clark's partner.

As we pulled into a lovely Quality Inn at eight thirty, a thermometer on a bank building read 95 degrees. Locals told us high temperatures like this are normal for summer in the valley, despite its northern location. Based upon riding ninety-six miles and climbing 4,300 feet, my cycling computer estimated we had each burned 4,200 calories. The smell of freshly baked chocolate chip cookies greeted us in the hotel lobby and reinvigorated our appetites. Despite consuming plenty of food and fluids all day long, we were ravenously hungry. We were gaining better appreciation for the nutritional requirements,

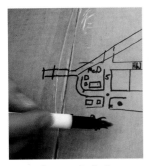

A Walmart clerk draws a map to Sunday's service

with more yet to learn. *Wow,* I thought. *Ninety-six miles is pretty good. I wonder if we can keep this up.* I also wondered how many calories we had really burned. We were carrying substantial loads in hot weather—and those variables weren't in the computer.

Our hotel's convenient location facilitated some late-night shopping at Super Walmart and our Sunday morning walk to a local church service. We were in a good place after a long but rewarding day. The church proved most friendly. We received a couple of invitations for food and fellowship, which we declined as checkout time and more mileage beckoned. We left with warm wishes and a DVD souvenir of the Snake River. We later regretted not taking more of a break as we soon discovered a challenging ride to higher altitudes ahead.

Horse country in Idaho

We headed out intending a relaxing recovery ride after yesterday's long haul. Our bodies were tired and the heat was again intense. Nevertheless, we plodded into Idaho along country roads dotted with farms and ranches. This was horse country and services were sparse. We quickly felt the extent of our fatigue. We stopped to rest and enjoy some snacks before firming up our itinerary. Our late start and unclear path forced us to resume after only a brief, inadequate respite.

Lapwai, Idaho

We reached Donald's Café in Lapwai, where the temperature read 100 degrees at suppertime. Locals offered conflicting advice for our evening ride. Some advocated the direct route, while others, citing past cyclist fatalities on the main road, encouraged us to take the longer route. The apologists for the safer route won out. Despite some additional mileage and only a few more hours of daylight, we headed toward a campground at the end of a very long climb using the alternative route on Adventure Cycling's maps.

We were awestruck by the beautiful sunset over the rolling hills and farmland as seen from the guardrail-less and winding Old Winchester Grade Road. The switchbacks on this narrow and lightly traveled road gave us the full panoramic view as we snaked our way up into the darkness. The long climb, in excess of 2,000 feet, was more than daylight would allow. Although the altitude provided incredible views of the sun's lengthy exodus from the western sky, we needed to climb several hundred more feet and travel who knew how many more miles to reach camping services.

Unfortunately, I had overestimated our ability to reach the campground before dark. I had paid more attention to the mileage on the map rather than the elevation, failing to discern the effect of the long, steep ascent. It was a lesson in map reading I would not soon forget. By nightfall, after donning headlamps, we were miles short of the campground even as we continued the ascent. New

Incredible sunset on the Old Winchester Grade Road

distractions had trumped our focus on fatigue from earlier in the day. The first was the breathtaking sunset. And then came the fear of surprise encounters with out-of-control vehicles careening along the windy road, the wild men driving them, or whatever other living creatures might spring, dart, lunge, creep, or crawl—or roar, growl, howl, snarl, or hiss—from the black unknown. And, as if those concerns weren't enough, steering our bicycles into the dark abyss merely feet to our right haunted us. As the darkness thickened, reality began to set in. Reaching the campground tonight was a fantasy. It was time to find somewhere else to pitch our tent.

I was so scared. The lack of guardrails on this road combined with the drop-off was downright frightful. We were now better able to control the bikes, but neither of us felt comfortable riding along the edge of this road in daylight. Then, after the sunset, we couldn't even see the edge. The puny beam of our headlamps was useless. Yet, Tim wouldn't stop. Either he thought the campground was around the next corner or he was being too particular on where to pitch the tent. The darker it got, the more afraid I became. I kept praying for God to make him stop, and finally he did. I was relieved. The next day, we discovered we were miles and hours from the campground.

We found a promising field set off from the road. We wheeled our bicycles up a dirt road and far enough into the field to be out of sight—at least from other people traveling on the road. Since we were still learning the camping routine, our setup took about ninety minutes. By midnight, we were lying on our backs in the tent, mesmerized by the ambiance of a warm night, a clear sky inundated with stars, and one another's company. As we gazed at the constellations, we could only be amazed at the beauty of this facet of God's creation. Our emotions had again come full circle. What a night! The temperature was perfect and we were nestled in a secluded perch that protected us from man and beast, or so we thought. The hair-raising uncertainty of our twilight ride had led to a warm, peaceful evening in a beautiful setting under a clear, star-filled sky. Life is good!

In the morning, we awoke to a beautiful hillside sunrise. We carefully and thoroughly cleaned up our makeshift campsite and packed our bikes. As we began wheeling them toward the Old Winchester Grade Road, suddenly, a middle-aged couple in a large pickup truck entered the tote road. The truck's speed and its revving engine suggested they were on a mission. And our own sense of guilt suggested we were the target. It was difficult to read their expressionless faces, but deep inside, I sensed confrontation looming. I could only surmise the landowners had come to see what we were doing on their land. Perhaps our site was not as secluded as we had thought. Or perhaps this was just a case of poor timing. With nervous smiles and a half-hearted wave, we walked our loaded bikes out of our spotless overnight hideaway. The stone-faced man immediately put his truck in reverse and left without word or gesture! I remain curious to this day who they were and what they were thinking.

Clearly, we were inexperienced tourists, but adventure cyclists nonetheless. In hindsight, it may have been better to knock on someone's door, looking for a tent-sized parcel of land, and risking an up-front confrontation with a nasty dog or an unwelcoming homeowner. Nevertheless, my lack of foresight resulted in a suspense-filled evening, an awesome star show, and a wonderful night's sleep. It was a happy ending—at least for that day.

6. Facing Our Fears

WE WERE SOON DEEP WITHIN IDAHO and continuing to approach the Continental Divide, although we assumed it was many days away. We were more familiar with both our bicycles and the daily routine that would help make us more efficient. We were also learning more about each other, for better or worse. Daily mileage expectations had become less important. Yesterday's planned recovery ride was anything but, yet we only logged forty miles at a speed of only seven and a half miles per hour. At that rate, it would take ten hours of riding to obtain our daily goal for mileage. For now, the terrain commanded our attention. We would worry about the adequacy of our daily mileage when and if we proved ourselves at hill climbing. It seemed doubtful we would be able to make it to the Atlantic, but there was so much to enjoy each day that long-range goals temporarily faded into the background.

Bicycling in Idaho felt different. We encountered isolated areas of hilly farmland with narrow, less-traveled roads. But we also rode on a major highway, with its speeding tractor trailers and precariously confining rumble strips. In the distance was our first sighting of snow-capped mountains since Mount Hood, reminding us that steeper and longer climbs lay ahead. Although we both relish a challenge, our confidence in our climbing abilities lagged. We had

Idaho

little experience in mountainous terrain, especially with a large load onboard. Could we handle the Rockies? Time would tell.

Midway through our eleventh day of riding, natural beauty surrounded us again. We crossed lovely farmland, branded with rolling hills and lush crops. Unripe wheat rippled in the wind like waves in the ocean, encapsulating narrow country roads. A friendly tailwind set the tone for our passage through this aesthetically pleasing area, boosting us up and down short hills until we arrived at the apex of a twelve-mile descent into Kamiah. As we cruised down the other side, an adjoining stream ushered us from a farming setting to what felt like backwoods.

We hadn't taken a day off since leaving the Pacific and were still reeling from yesterday's twilight climb. The map forewarned of a more desolate stretch of road ahead with longer distances between services. Coasting into town seemed like a fitting end to the day. So, despite another short day of fifty-four miles, we restocked on carbohydrates and calories at the Pizza Factory and found overnight accommodations at the Lewis and Clark Resort.

Entering the Wild

On the following day, we entered an even more remote area, Clearwater National Forest, along US Route 12. The heat wave of the past week had abated. The adjacent mountain creeks and the accompanying Clearwater River provided pleasant sights along this densely forested stretch. Full evergreen trees spiked skyward on the neighboring hills, creating a rich green hue while pointing to the clear, deep blue sky. The bright sun helped accentuate the vibrant colors, the magnificent area, and the pleasant day. Various waterfalls, labeled as "creeks," but pronounced like "cricks," trickled from hills on the north side of the road and crossed under the road to deposit their clear mountain waters into the larger river for passage to lower altitudes. Several intriguing wooden footbridges crossed the rushing river rapids to connect hikers to trails on either side. The river hosted both fly-fishers and more adventuresome whitewater rafters.

Tumble Creek   *Footbridge*

As we climbed along US Route 12, we were joined by logging trucks, vehicles in a hurry to nowhere, and other cyclists. One couple rolling toward us caught my attention. They were using a trailer to carry their gear, and I noticed the guy was carrying all of the gear. This seemed like a prime opportunity to lighten my own load. Tim had already suggested earlier that he carry more of my stuff. Given the upcoming climbs and the difficulty of ascending with a heavy load, I gladly gave him some heavier items in exchange for lighter ones.

We stopped for lunch at a rustic roadside cabin in Lowell. After eating, we couldn't help but visit the cabin's inner room, which sported a crude taxidermy display of various specimens of wildlife. On one wall, a game bird flaunted its midflight plumage. A small pelt and deer antlers surrounded it. To the side, as if standing watch out the window, was a deer head mounted on a plaque. Two more deer heads adorned the back wall, along with an elk or caribou head, and the sprawled pelt of a large feline. A small bear with beady, sunken, marble eyes and a drawn mouth stood on its hind feet in the corner, particularly notable due to its scrawny and harmless appearance. In fact, all of these stuffed creatures seemed harmless, if not pitiful. But they were all dead. There is no savage, wild, or fearsome in lifelessness. Without a heartbeat, those qualities could live only in one's imagination. In mine, they can thrive.

I grew up in Maine, where the black bear is the mascot of the flagship campus of the state's university system. I know just a little about black bears, but next to nothing about the larger and more fearsome grizzly. I really did not want any close encounters with hungry or threatened animals, as we were ill-equipped, ill-prepared, and naïve when it came to wildlife. Our new surroundings, coupled with our conversation with a retired Iowa State professor, reminded us we were now in the wild.

The friendly professor was enjoying another long stretch of what he referred to as primitive camping. He had been camping on remote trails in the Clearwater National Forest for forty-five straight days. I took the opportunity to learn more about the perils of encountering dangerous species, not knowing what lay ahead. He told me he had never had encounters in his campsite. "Keep a clean campsite," he said. "Leave no food or trash strewn about." He had seen three cougars and one grizzly on area trails. With a large, powerful canister of bear spray by his side, his adventures in the wild were helping him whittle away at his list of things to do before he dies. Although our journey intrigued him because he aspired to bicycle across the country in earlier days, he had waited too long and became, as he put it, "old and fat." However, clearly, our spirit of adventure was more easily satisfied than his. Armed with bear spray or not, we wouldn't be hiking in those woods anytime soon.

Climbing to New Heights

When we reached the climb to Lolo Pass, which would usher us from Idaho to Montana, we still doubted our ability to climb the Rockies. We were in uncharted waters. I had never been west of Nashville, Tennessee, before our plane flight a few weeks earlier. Other than glancing at some of the peaks from the airplane window as we flew over them, my understanding of the Rockies came from what I had seen on television and what others had told me. Call it the fear of the unknown, but my perception of what we would face climbing into the mountains was left to my imagination. A rather intimidating notion loomed, despite the elevation data provided by the Adventure Cycling maps.

I had some familiarity with the Rockies, having lived in Colorado for twenty years where the peaks are very high. In those days, however, I was a runner. I understood thinner air at high altitudes could reduce an athlete's ability to generate power. But I simply had no idea what cycling in these heights would be like. At least on this day, I was looking forward to finding out.

Almost imperceptibly, we had begun the climb at the start of the day. We would spend a day and a half getting to the steeper portion of the climb. We resumed our journey up US Route 12, a designated National Scenic Byway. The terrain, deficient shoulders, and sharp, attention-getting turns made cycling this road more challenging when traffic appeared. Traveling west to east, Route 12 is a 110-mile, 3,800-foot ascent, ultimately destined for Lolo Pass. Simply the word "pass" induced excitement, if not intrigue or outright fear. However, that challenge would come tomorrow.

Fifty-five miles into the day, we reached the Wilderness Gateway Campground, where we would pitch our tent for the evening. In this remote national forest, we had no cell coverage. Isolation can be both a blessing and a curse, but it usually fosters greater self-reliance. It was comforting, however, to have one another. This was a new phenomenon for us, and it was exciting. The love we felt for one another was a powerful antidote to fear and anxiety.

Given our earlier discussions with the good professor, our chosen campsite was far enough away from neighboring campsites to ensure privacy, but close enough to garner support should we need it. Not much activity could be found in this heavily wooded campground. In fact, some of the campsites with recreational vehicles seemed lifeless. Nevertheless, there were a few RVs with people merely a sprint away. We felt more comfortable when a group of teenage cyclists arrived and pitched tents between the deeper woods and us. Surely, they would create enough hubbub to keep unwelcome furry visitors away from our campsite.

I have to admit being a bit jealous of those people in the RVs. They had comfortable beds, plenty of food and drink, coverage from the wild, and better toilet facilities. There we were, after riding fifty-five uphill miles, stuck in a tent in the wild.

But then I considered what they didn't have: simplicity, adventure, and the thrill of it all. It didn't take me long to get over my jealousy.

So, there we were, at a campground on US Route 12 in Idaho. The next morning, we would be going through the pass that brought Lewis and Clark across the Rockies to the West Coast. Camping in that environment was fun. We used our water-boiling stove to convert freeze-dried beef stroganoff into dinner and instant oatmeal into breakfast. Temperatures were cooler than we had experienced on our trip. Snuggling in our sleeping bags inside our cozy tent kept us warm enough for a good sleep during a peaceful evening.

Camp Bishop, Gateway Wilderness Campground

We awoke the next morning in a cool, damp tent. Heavy dew, cooler temperatures, and our failure to use the tent covering, or so-called fly, chilled us. Just two days ago, we were cycling in 100-degree heat. On this morning, we could see our breath. Traveling as light as we did, we had taken a calculated risk that we would not need heavy clothing. A lightweight fleece and hot chocolate proved sufficient to ward off the cool morning. Once back on the road, we knew that our increased heart rates and the powerful July sun would soon return us to a comfortable riding temperature.

Tearing down camp took longer than expected. Our teenage neighbors from the metro New York area, led by an experienced cyclist appropriately named "Miles," beat us out of camp by a large margin. Miles had bicycled through Lolo before and gave us a sneak preview. The road would be similar to what we had experienced the day before, but the climb would become more difficult as we approached the top. Logging trucks would share a more narrow and winding road with us. But the arrival at the summit's visitor center would be well worth the climb. Debbie and I knew we would be facing a test. Our maps indicated a 2,800-foot climb. Butterflies fluttered within. If we made it to the top early enough, we might make it all the way to Missoula. There was a forty-mile stretch of mostly declining altitude on the other side. But first came the climb.

> I was anxious about riding up to Lolo Pass. I really didn't want to leave the campsite. I didn't know if I could make it over the pass. But I also knew there was no turning back. Once again, self-talk and prayer renewed my motivation to ride.

Four hours after awakening, we finally hit the road. Debbie later admitted to stalling in the morning due to the specter of the upcoming climb. I wasn't about to chide her, because I had my own reservations.

Again, we rode alongside a gorgeous river, winding through the strikingly beautiful evergreen forest. The magnificent scenery along the Lochsa River escorted us to lunch, transforming a long gradual climb into a leisurely ride on a splendid day. We stopped to eat and

Lochsa River

replenish our fluids at Lochsa Lodge's lovely log cabin dining room. The architecture within, including a high ceiling, log beam supports, central fireplace, and plenty of natural light, dished up an ambiance teeming with grandeur. An old player piano and a window-side table overlooking the beautiful forest garnished the memorable setting and our delectable lunch.

By mid-afternoon, we had embarked on the more serious climb to the top of Lolo Pass. When the grade steepened, I started counting off each 100 feet of elevation as encouragement to Debbie. We slowed to a crawl up Route 12, which was now shaped more like a pretzel than a major US highway as it snaked its way around the

Cycling through the Clearwater National Forest in Idaho

Climbing made easy in picturesque Idaho

mountain. The higher altitude rewarded us with lookout points over a ravine on the north side of the road. However, despite the fatigue and the slow pace, we weren't about to stop. We knew we would have great difficulty restarting, just as we learned back in Oregon on day two.

The road had a distinct mountain pass feel, twisting around the hills and leaving the rivers behind. The tree cover began to thin as we neared the top. We continued to slither up the road, clinging to the edge, given its inadequate shoulder and passing lane. Trucks and motorcycles rumbled by, adding to the stress and tension. Eventually, we crept to the top and arrived at the closed Lolo Pass Visitor Center.

Even at that point in our trip, the day's 2,800-foot climb was working us into better riding shape. But more than the physical benefit, accomplishing the steep climb together was a psychological victory, a confidence booster, and a bonding experience. We had rendered the paralyzing grip of the morning's fears and anxiety

Typical traffic and shoulders on US Route 12 in Idaho

powerless. The roaring lion within was really just a harmless, playful pussycat.

We were still only 5,200 feet above sea level. We had not yet reviewed the maps to see how much higher we would climb, but we expected the Rockies would be much higher than this altitude. Our minds had already begun to concoct scenarios that resurrected anxiety. The fear of the unknown had become a chisel, no sooner put in its case than to reemerge to whittle away at our psyche once again.

Most fears have some basis in reality, but we usually give them too much power. Everybody has different things holding him back. Some handle fear and anxiety better than others. But everyone has the opportunity to come face to face with discovery. The encounter itself helps define adventure, when we must overcome resistance to venture into the unknown and to discover the unfathomable blessings in what lies ahead. The moment of truth is fraught with peril and fear, fueled by adrenaline and thrill, and fulfilled with growth and satisfaction. If it weren't, life would be dull. Without some adventure in our lives, we would become entrenched and unchanging, and begin to endure a slow death. A day will arrive when the sands of time have sifted through, and what will you have to show for it? I had come to appreciate these truths more and more in the past several months. And certain facets of our bike ride reflected them well.

Down the Other Side

The uninterrupted climb had taken a toll. We rested despite the cooler, breezy air that accompanied the sunset. Although the scenery was a worthwhile reward for our efforts, the area felt more like forest than a mountaintop. There were no lengthy overlooks; rather, conifers blanketed the views in all directions. With the visitor center closed, the grounds were vacant. We reviewed the external exhibits, which taught us the history of the region and described what was ahead. A large-scale map of Montana was particularly intriguing. We would begin to cross the lengthy state momentarily.

When we were ready to resume, we realized our journey up Lolo Pass had not come without consequences. Debbie had some difficulty restarting.

> I was so tired from the climb. When mounting my bicycle to resume our ride, I dropped it twice. Along with its heavy load, the bicycle and I crashed to the ground. It was really more humiliating than painful thanks to the cushioning effect of the stuffed rear panniers.
>
> My knee was already a little sore from the climb; I was worn out and wanted to stop for the night. We would need to coast down to warmer heights and find some shelter for the evening.

I had developed a limp from a sore Achilles tendon. I wondered, *What if either one of us develops a chronic pain and we have to stop touring for awhile, or are unable to continue?* It was a nasty thought, frankly horrifying. We had invested so much, were experiencing life anew, and so much remained. Aborting the process of discovering our land and ourselves on this fantastic journey would be tragic.

Outfitted with some warmer clothes, we finally left Lolo Pass at dusk and entered the largest state on our route. Montana greeted us with three cautionary props that slowed us on what we had hoped would be a screaming descent. The first was an oversized yellow sign warning of loose gravel and urging caution. The sign was most likely intended for motorized vehicles, but loose gravel can easily topple a bicycle, particularly at higher speeds. Almost immediately, a second sign followed, explaining that white roadside crosses would mark sites of traffic fatalities across the entire state. A small, solitary, white cross stood soberly next to the sign. And, finally, deer at random intervals along our descent, about two fistfuls in all, stood at the ready. They were as still as lawn ornaments, yet poised to dart into the road or deeper into the woods should the appropriate stimulus trigger their nervous bodies to spring into action. With caution as our watchword, the stage was set for the proprietor of The Lodge at Lolo Hot Springs to unwittingly exploit our overactive imaginations and our own jumpiness.

With daylight waning and wildlife wandering, we were glad to reach his establishment after just a few miles of descent. Despite its dot on the map, Lolo Hot Springs appeared to be no more than a couple of businesses on either side of the road. We hadn't seen a home since entering the state—only trees, deer, and US Route 12. In this setting, The Lodge's attractive sign and complex on the left immediately drew us.

We went into the office and discovered we had just entered the mountain time zone. The motel was about to close for the evening. They had a room for $129, which was more than we wanted to pay. The proprietor promoted twenty-four-hour "free" access to the hot springs, which were housed within his complex. He said a bear, three moose, some deer, and a wolf frequented the property. The bear, he claimed, was often seen on the back western side of the complex where our room faced. He assured us the wildlife would be more afraid of us than we would be of them. Lacking the energy and willpower to be choosy about our room or its price, and perhaps intrigued by the unusual attractions, we immediately signed up for the room. Darkness had already fallen and we weren't about to take the chance we would need to camp out in the wild. Little did we know that more affordable cabins at less than half the cost sat right across the road.

The room was impressive with its beautiful, finished log motif. This was a golden nugget unearthed in the middle of the forest. We ate dinner at the adjoining bar, where we were reunited with our teenage neighbors from the prior evening. They were destined for Portsmouth, New Hampshire, expecting to complete their entire journey in forty-seven days. Debbie and I wondered whether our thirty-five-year age difference would prevent us from keeping up with them. Pride can be an insidious foe. We would face more challenges ahead than mere aerobic capacity or muscle strength.

Debbie coaxed me into the hot springs before midnight. I am typically skeptical of such things, but a warm soaking certainly would relax the muscles. I also felt obliged because I knew the hot springs were not really free. The real treat, however, was the clean, modern, and lovely room with its comfortable bed. It was so inviting that we regretted not being able to stay longer. Despite none of the advertised wildlife sightings, we left the premises the next morning feeling we had received fair value for our stay. Sometimes, the special blessings of life come about in unexpected ways.

Outside was another phenomenal day. The sun was beaming and the sky bluer than blue. This was our first taste of the original "big sky," and we loved it. The soreness in my ankle had vanished. I thought it rather amazing because I'd had difficulty pedaling down Lolo Pass just hours earlier. Thank goodness I had been able to coast much of the way. Debbie insisted our late-night soaking at Lolo Hot Springs healed my ankle. Her knee was also better. I must admit it was difficult to argue with the positive effect of the warm springs.

But another health issue was looming. We both had some significant saddle sores. Debbie was developing what would soon become
the mother of saddle sores. Since Walla Walla six days ago, we had
been cleansing and monitoring one another's sores religiously. We
had also been cleaning, sun-baking, and rotating our shorts daily.
But what we had not done—yet—was to stay off the bicycles for more
than an evening. We also hadn't sought any medical treatment.
Debbie's painful sore was clearly more than skin deep. We assumed
it would soon come to the surface and resolve itself. And we were
giving it time to do so.

We passed snow-covered Lolo Peak and pedaled to Missoula,
a pleasant, bicyclist-friendly college town. We stopped to maintain
bicycles, restock supplies, and do laundry—the conventional way.
The wobble in my front tire had become more pronounced since we
left Seaside at the start of our trip. The local bike shop looked the
bicycles over just before they closed and made only minor adjustments. They thought the weight of my load was excessive for the
bicycle, causing the wheel to fall out of true. But after traveling for
700 miles through hilly terrain, I wasn't inclined to change strategy. This answer didn't seem right. The bike had performed well
and still seemed solid. Besides, what was I going to do? Everything I
was carrying was there for a reason. I wasn't ready to ship anything
back and I certainly didn't want Debbie carrying more weight. The
bicycle shop seemed more interested in closing for the day than in
repairing an imperfect wheel. There would be more shops ahead.

I was more interested in gathering intelligence on the grizzly
bear population. Whether influenced by the University of Montana's
grizzly bear mascot or haunted by our earlier conversation with the
good professor in Idaho, I wondered where the bears roamed and
how many more days we would risk encountering one. When the
salesman told me we would be clear in just one day, I was incredu-
lous. We hadn't experienced high mountains yet. *Are we really that
close to the edge of the wilderness?* I wondered. When he told me
the eastern two-thirds of the state was wide-open space, I listened
intently, but deep within, my own misconceptions produced more

skepticism. I thought Montana was a mountainous state. Confused, I left the bike shop not knowing what to expect.

Of even more concern was Debbie's condition. She refused to seek a medical opinion. Looking at the map, I thought we would be several days away from the next hospital once we left Missoula. And I wasn't sure how difficult the riding might be. We had already decided to forgo the longer scenic route in order to trim 300 miles and some additional mountain climbing from our trip. We had long since learned that the shortest distance between two points is a straight line. What lay ahead was totally foreign to me and seemed very sparsely populated. What if Debbie needed emergency treatment? Her condition really bothered me. Her sore seemed to be getting worse rather than better. And I could sense the anxiety in her.

> My butt hurt so much. When I rode my bike, it felt like I was sitting on a large marble—we used to call the big ones "poppers." Pain would shoot into my midsection unless I positioned myself on the bicycle just right. I assumed this would pass as these types of things always do; however, I had never really had this condition before.
>
> Inside, I was also doubtful about the whole trip. I didn't want to stop for fear we would never resume, or if we did, we wouldn't make it back in time for work. Although I didn't share this with Tim at the time, I figured I could just find an airport somewhere and fly home. He could finish the trip by himself. Later, I realized that such a turn of events would have negated one of the gifts of marriage: togetherness through the good times as well as the bad.

A few miles down the road from Missoula the following morning, Debbie broke down and cried. Not only did her sore hurt, but we had both also been through a lot in the last few weeks. The trip was a fanciful delight before embarking, but it was now work. I really didn't like leaving the services of Missoula with her in this condition. We would need to cover about eighty miles to make it to a motel for the evening and it appeared there was little to nothing in between.

The gorgeous scenery of western Montana

We had achieved daily mileage like that only once before in our trip, nearly a week ago. If the journey continued to be hilly, we would never make it that far—especially on a sore behind. But Debbie was determined to keep going. I assumed she knew her body better than I did, but I also wasn't going to let this go untreated indefinitely. Great Falls was the next major service center on the map. We'd need to reassess her condition then. Somehow, she collected herself for what would become one of the most inspiring days yet.

Big Sky Country

Whoever coined the term "Big Sky Country" to describe Montana knew what they were talking about. The impressive beauty and grandeur of western Montana were everywhere we looked. There were surprisingly few snow-capped mountains, but rather rounded peaks with a bluish hue. The dense tree cover found on either side of Lolo Pass had disappeared. We now saw hills with sparse coverage

Anglers enjoy the Blackfoot River   *Cattle graze in western Montana*

of evergreens against a deep blue sky, creating a unique signature denoting Montana landscape. Sparkling rivers invited anglers and rafters, providing yet another magnificent facet to the area's appeal.

To make matters even better, a strong wind chased us as if ordered up from On High. It was a breath of fresh air breathing new life into our journey. Somehow, the physical and mental challenges took a backseat. I could sense Debbie's state of mind improve as we pedaled into this incredible landscape. The unforgettable day's scenery was so breathtaking that nothing else mattered.

As if to put an end to the question of whether we had arrived in "God's Country," eagles soared overhead in awe-inspiring fashion, leaving us spellbound, moved to the verge of tears. The eagles were a testimony to going with the current, not pushing against circumstances in life, but using current conditions to reach new heights. They soared with such ease and beauty that we just stopped and gazed at our nation's symbol. These birds also served as powerful reminders of God's presence in our lives and His

Debbie captures an unforgettable moment

Big Sky Country

blessing on our trip. Let us explain why eagles have such a special place in our hearts.

Faith and Eagles

When I was in my thirties, I encountered the same Bible verse four times in two weeks. These sightings materialized amid a period of years when I was seeking, and asking God for, a godly spouse. The first occurred when I was on vacation in Connecticut. After a gym workout, my cousin was driving us back to his house when he said, "What's that verse?"

"What verse?" I asked.

He pointed to a tractor trailer in front of us with a picture of a large eagle as well as the inscription *Isaiah 40:31* painted on its side. I told him I did not readily know that verse, but I would look it up when we got back to the house. I was thinking it might be of help to him or his son. So, when we returned to his home, I read them the verse.

But those who wait on the Lord
Shall renew their strength;
They shall mount up with wings like eagles,
They shall run and not be weary,
They shall walk and not faint.

—Isaiah 40:31

The next day, I went to visit a friend in another part of Connecticut. John was a very spiritual friend. I was explaining the struggle I was having with the lack of female companionship in my life. In the midst of sharing some thoughts about my situation, he quoted the same passage—Isaiah 40:31. I thought it rather interesting he would share this verse. I commented, in passing, I had seen the reference to it on a trailer the day before.

Upon returning to Maine, I saw this verse again a day or two later. In the middle of a prayer one evening, I inexplicably felt compelled to go to the kitchen to check the calendar. There was only one verse on the face of this calendar, and it immediately struck me. My stomach sunk—and then my heartbeat quickened. It was Isaiah 40:31—again! Even though I had seen this verse before on that same calendar, this time it overtook me. It couldn't have stood out more if it were a flashing neon light.

Hey, wait a minute! I thought. *This verse is intended for me. But why?* I was already frustrated because I had been praying for years for a companion. I thought I had been very patient and had already waited long enough. With this third sighting, I finally understood that God was speaking to me, but I still did not know what He was saying.

Several days later, as if to remove any doubt God was speaking to me, I came across a fourth revelation. I traveled north to take my mother on a vacation in Canada. On our return trip through the remote Miramichi River region of New Brunswick, we stopped in a small town named Doaktown. We visited a small, rustic museum. While Mom was busy talking with an attendant, I was immediately drawn to an old hymnal that sat on an old organ. I walked over and picked the hymnal up to see how old it was, checking inside for a copyright date. Then, I randomly opened it to the middle. To my astonishment, I was staring at a hymn that filled both pages, the sole words of which were the words of Isaiah 40:31—verbatim! Despite a lifetime of church attendance, I had not realized such a hymn even existed. I immediately closed the book and walked away with no doubt these sightings were divine appointments.

Isaiah 40:31 began to shape my perspective on all things. It was a constant reminder of God's presence and call for patience. I would periodically see replicas of the eagle everywhere, whereas beforehand they might simply have blended in with their surroundings and gone unnoticed. And, of course, when I saw one, I would always think of this verse. From time to time, I would see an eagle flying high above my home along the Penobscot River in Bangor, Maine. I even spotted this verse highlighted on the walls of two nonprofits I have supported for years, including TheHopeLine.

One day, the development director for TheHopeLine took an unusual interest in my e-mail address, which includes the reference to this verse. When he asked why I used this verse in my e-mail address, for some reason I took the time out of a very busy day to explain the history chronicled above. With keen interest, he told me that another supporter of the organization owns a trailer with this verse on it. Could this have been the same trailer I saw years ago? A few years later, this donor sold the trailer to another individual who is also a supporter of TheHopeLine. As Debbie and I were planning our wedding, I asked the development director if he could obtain a photograph of this trailer for our use as a prop at our reception. When the trailer's previous owner learned of our story, he not only sent a large, color print of the tractor trailer, but he also sent us a book entitled *The Eagle Story* as a wedding gift. According to this individual, whom we had never met, *The Eagle Story*, which teaches some spiritual truths using the attributes of the eagle, changed his life.

The legacy of Isaiah 40:31 grew when I met author and life coach Dan Miller, who is a self-professed student of eagles and, in fact, uses one in his business logo. He highlights the attributes of eagles in his writing. The name of the program I enrolled in with Mr. Miller was the Eagles Club. Months later, another chapter in my eagle story was written when I proposed to Debbie overlooking Eagle Lake.

> In early 2009, when Tim first told me about how God had spoken to him through Isaiah 40:31 fourteen years earlier, I thought, *Wow, that's unusual.* Little did I know my own dose of Isaiah 40:31 revelations was about to visit me. The following weekend, I attended a Christian women's retreat in Cape Cod, Massachusetts. During a break, I found a name card for sale with my name, Deborah, on it. The card contained the word "industrious" and, fittingly, Isaiah 40:31. Later, all the women received a note card on which to write some encouraging words to someone who had made a difference in their lives. The card they gave me had Isaiah 40:31 on it. Naturally, I chose to send the card to Tim. These two cards encouraged me that God was at work while I was waiting for my own special companion.

So, when we saw eagles flying majestically overhead in western Montana, what else were we going to think? They gave us plenty of inspiration to keep pedaling. We also had perhaps the best scenery yet. We traveled along the Blackfoot River, a bastion for fishing and rafting, surrounded in the distance by grand mountain ranges, some sprinkled and some splashed with evergreen trees. The crisp and colossal blue sky overseeing acres of open space brought it all together in the Master Architect's impression of "The Big Sky."

The rumble strips and high-speed traffic on Route 200 were not going to deter us. We even received special encouragement late in the day when a man walked across the parking lot at a rest stop and offered us two cold bottles of water from his cooler. Seventy-eight miles through a picture-book setting landed us in Lincoln's Sportsman Motel. True to the largeness of the state and its magnificent big sky, there were three double beds and a fireplace. After supper at the Montanan next door, we set Debbie's medical

The Continental Divide!

concern on the mantle and enjoyed a restful sleep. After a day like that, somehow life's troubles did not seem so insurmountable. We couldn't do anything about it anyway. Tomorrow's journey was even longer, but with another surprise just down the road.

Over the Top

Great Falls seemed too far away, but an early start would help maximize our riding time. The direct route appeared to be almost ninety miles, but the map recommended a longer one. We would have sixty to seventy miles before we came to the fork in the road. Before that, there appeared to be a whole lot of nothing. Yesterday's ride didn't seem too hilly, although we ended the day 1,300 feet higher than we'd started it. If I believed what the bike shop salesman back in Missoula told me, this day should offer flatter terrain.

Just fifteen miles into the day, we arrived at Rogers Pass and the Continental Divide. When I saw the sign, I was shocked. *You're kidding!* I thought. *Where are the Rockies?* We had seen so few snow-covered mountains. Climbing through the Rockies had been much easier than expected and, other than Lolo Pass, did not seem like climbing at all. Rogers Pass only stands 5,600 feet above sea level.

Unbeknownst to us, we had been ascending and fast approaching the beginning of the downhill ride east. Another friendly tailwind had shrouded the climb. But we weren't about to get cocky. After all, there were 3,000 miles to go.

Arriving at this landmark would not have surprised most bicycle tourists, but it did surprise us. We had done so little pre-trip planning and were so busy with other aspects of the trip that we hadn't reviewed the map in detail, except when making immediate decisions about when and where to turn. But sure enough, there it was on the map: the Continental Divide!

The phantom climb up Rogers Pass seemed insignificant, but the descent was a treat. The eastern side of the pass was steeper with some switchbacks. My fearless wife, who sees no use for brakes when descending, flew around the curves and down the mountain. After all, why use brakes and spoil the fun after you worked so hard to get up the hill? Wasn't this the reward? Of course, she does have a good point!

Debbie descends Rogers Pass

It's just that I was looking forward to spending the evening with her in a motel room, not the emergency room. With her sore rear end unresolved, one way or the other, she was bound to get to a hospital. As would become our custom with steep descents, I caught up with her at the bottom.

We pulled away from the Continental Divide and proceeded toward a still distant land flatter than we could have imagined. For miles, we faced a series of rolling hills averaging about 200 feet in rise. You might think of them as moguls for Sasquatch or Paul Bunyan, whichever one wears size-1,000 ski boots. These were not difficult to climb, just annoying because they slowed our progress toward Great Falls. We continued for hours in the heat along a service-less stretch

Debbie descends Rogers Pass – the full view!

Leaving the Rockies behind on Route 200 in Montana

of Highway 200. High-speed traffic whizzed by as we negotiated a variety of rumble strips and crested knoll after knoll.

Eventually the hills became fewer and farther between until we approached the plains around Great Falls and the Missouri River. The mountains that had enveloped us were shrinking, fading into the distance. We traveled through "Prime Beef Country," or so the sign said. The land and accompanying vistas were vast and expansive. As hard as it was to believe, the Rockies had disappeared from our rearview mirrors. Climbs and descents of any magnitude now lay thousands of miles and several weeks to the east.

Our eighty-eight-mile day through the Continental Divide was satisfying but far from easy. The wind on the eastern side of the divide was decidedly against us. Route 200 was not a bicycle-friendly road. And we were isolated from services for much of the day. This would have been a very lonely day without one another, as in fact most of them would be. Debbie was absolutely exhausted and really struggled with the last ten miles. She was dealing with such physical stress on her body that she stopped every mile or two to pass fluid. It was going straight through her. Her drive to continue was impressive. I knew when I married Debbie that she loved to push herself in physical endeavors, but this was amazing—especially considering her sore butt. For a guy who enjoys physical activities like bicycling, Debbie is a treasure. To be married to her makes her a one-in-a-million treasure.

By dusk, we had made our way into the streets of Great Falls. The next day would be Sunday. We took special care to find accommodations within walking distance of a church. Spotting a Dairy Queen just after dark was reassuring. A couple who served Dairy Queen ice cream cakes at their wedding would certainly be passionate enough about Dairy Queen to find comfort there in unfamiliar territory. We quizzed some of the patrons about local churches and motels. One helpful individual borrowed the store's phone directory and helped us out. There just happened to be a church a block away. Fifteen minutes later, we located the Quality Inn, within walking distance of the church.

The next day would also be our first rest day. Great Falls would become a haven, a staging area, and a crossroads for us, with Debbie's saddle sore center stage. A time of rest, healing, strategy, and decision-making was upon us.

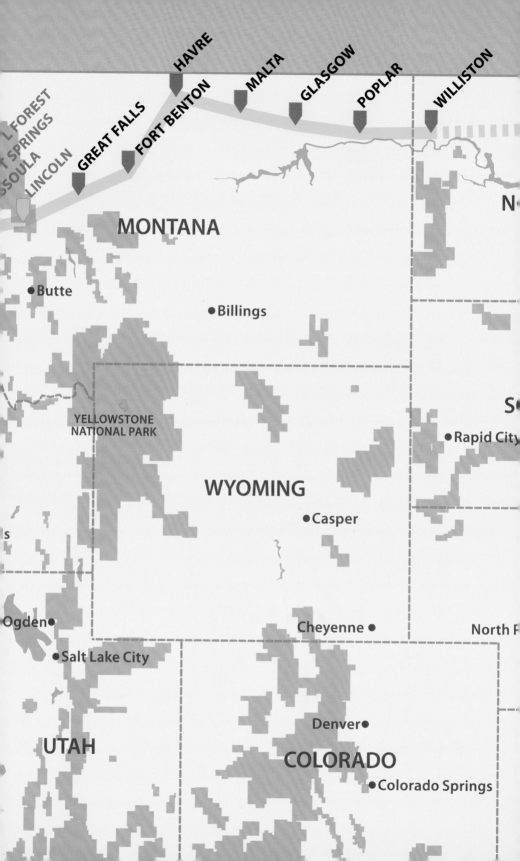

7. We Can Do This

WE WERE HOPEFUL THE NAME GREAT FALLS was not a premonition. We had come too far to stop now, but we needed to regroup. We suffered from saddle sores. Debbie took first prize with her lump. It might have been the size of one of Mom's dumplings, but the texture was more like that of a golf ball. She needed to see a doctor. We also needed to connect with loved ones and friends. And we had other matters to tend to. The blog needed more work. Our bicycles needed some repairs. We needed to plot our route out of Montana and reassess our potential for the entire trip. But, most importantly, our spent bodies needed to recover. They were tired and sore.

Recovery and Renewal

Sunday at church was reinvigorating. The senior pastor of forty-four years at the Fairview Baptist Church welcomed us warmly and escorted us to a Sunday school class. At seventy-five years of age, he had been married for fifty-four years, yet was as vivacious as a twenty-one-year-old. He was refreshing. Locals at the church advised us on travel routes out of Montana. Our adventure intrigued the friendly people, who wanted to help.

During the service, we witnessed several young people dedicate their lives to Jesus Christ. A momentous occasion like that excites me because I know what a positive impact it will have. People's lives change. They set a new direction and will soon discover a new set of tools for getting there. Others with whom they associate will also benefit. I remember my own conversion experience. I committed my life to Christ on November 18, 1966, at age eight. My father died just three months later. Knowing God has been a source of stability and growth since childhood. I am thankful that God reached me before my time of great need. I have learned that He sees around corners I cannot.

Early in my adult life, I had some challenging times and loneliness. In my mid-twenties, I was abruptly fired from a professional job—unjustifiably, or at least I thought so. Shortly thereafter, I suffered a marriage proposal rejection. A long and lonely search for female companionship ensued. For years, I lived with loneliness and unfulfilled longing. I learned, however, that God is near to the brokenhearted, and ultimately His ways are better than my ways. That truth was hammered home in glorious fashion when I married Debbie.

After church, we used the remainder of the day to rest and relax. We really needed it. Businesses were closed anyway. We enjoyed a leisure afternoon at a local park and walked the streets of downtown Great Falls.

On Monday, after an unsuccessful bid to schedule an appointment with a doctor (their earliest slot was in August), we walked to a medical "quick clinic" several miles away to have Debbie's saddle sore evaluated. The diagnosis was a perineal abscess. The physician assistant tried to lance and drain the abscess, but was unsuccessful. He referred Debbie to a gynecologist, whom she would see on Tuesday.

Monday was also bicycle repair day. The Knicker Biker was a short walk from the motel. After a quick evaluation, the mechanic recommended that he true both wheels on our bikes. I also asked him to replace my brake pads. With a heavier load and my more cautious riding style on descents, my pads had worn much more than Debbie's had. Also, our hands had been experiencing numbness and tingling due to the constant pressure of riding. Debbie's tingling seemed worse than mine did, so we had her bars double-wrapped and purchased a better pair of gloves to relieve some of the pressure. The service and the value rendered at the Knicker Biker were outstanding.

We also filtered through our belongings and set aside some excess baggage destined for home. After some negotiations, I was successful in convincing Debbie to ship back some of her makeup. Among the other items selected were used maps, the DVD given to us in Clarkston, extra clothing, and a belt. A visit to the nearby post office ensured our load would be ten pounds lighter in the days ahead—that was all we could muster.

Debbie seemed ready to hit the road already, but we weren't going anywhere until we addressed her medical issue. Even for this apprentice husband, some things came naturally. It was time to take charge. Debbie wasn't thinking the issue through. If her infection spread and we were days away from quality medical treatment, we would be risking a more serious condition. And if we didn't see any improvement, her traveling experience would be miserable. No, we were going to stay until her condition improved—like it or not. With a population of 60,000 and a major US air base, Great Falls offered the best services for many miles and days to come. We needed expert help, and we could find it here.

On Tuesday, we checked out of the motel, optimistic about a successful visit to the doctor's office. A warm, friendly nurse practitioner also tried to drain Debbie's abscess, but without success. She recommended that it be drained before Debbie resumed riding. She gave her some antibiotics and painkillers, and recommended we check back later in the week.

We were disappointed. When would the abscess be ready to drain? The uncertainty frustrated us. We were stuck, and it was an awful feeling—at least until we accepted it. We checked back into the Quality Inn. We were now losing valuable days from our allotment. Was our dream of making it across the country slipping through our hands as we sat in Great Falls unable to move?

We chose instead to dwell on the positive. We were reconnecting with family and friends and adding content to the blog. And, slowly, our bodies were getting much needed rest. Sores were clearing up (except for Debbie's stubborn one), muscles were regenerating, and minds were relaxing. The leisurely break was a godsend.

We also finally had extra time to plan. We hadn't done enough of that to date. We wanted to merge our current route with the Northern Tier route of the Adventure Cycling Route Network across the United States. The Northern Tier would bring us into New England, where we lived. We had two alternatives for traveling east, with the Missouri River watershed separating the two. We could either go north of the watershed or south, but either route would take days until they reunited just west of Williston, North Dakota.

We had heard enough advice already that suggested each of these routes had its challenges. Services were sparse on either route, but particularly so on the southern option. Locals warned us about the perils of traveling through several areas on the northern option, citing alcohol abuse and crazy kids. It was difficult to discern whether this was providential caution or simply old-fashioned prejudice and bigotry. With Debbie's sore bottom and the daily mileage needed to navigate this region, it seemed important to stay in motels.

> While Tim was planning our route out of Montana, I had made contact with my good friend Laurie Hegstad, who, with husband, Tim, lived just outside of Williston, North Dakota. Laurie described another type of lawlessness in her area. There was an oil boom in North Dakota. Migrant workers were taking over campgrounds and setting up makeshift campsites. The more affluent, or perhaps civilized, among these workers had claimed all motel accommodations west of Minot. I really didn't want to stay in a "man camp"—I wouldn't have felt safe, even with Tim by my side.
>
> Laurie further described commercial and oversized vehicles speeding up and down US Route 2 to support oil operations. The Williston area was not as attractive as it once was for bicycle tourists. It had instead become an industrial worksite. Laurie invited us for an overnight stay and a special transport around the entire region, and highly recommended we accept for our own safety. Safety aside, I was really looking forward to seeing Laurie. I hadn't seen her in years.

As I considered Debbie's phone conversation with Laurie, I thought, *Would hitching a ride somehow invalidate our cross-country trip, assuming we will be able to make it all the way across? Would we be excluded from some honorary club of cross-country cyclists, if such club exists? Who keeps score of these things? And can we afford to spend more time visiting with people after being stuck in Great Falls for several days?* This last question would come up again, as Debbie had relatives and I had friends in the Midwest.

We wrestled with these questions, but it became clear what we should do. To my knowledge, nobody was keeping score, there was no club, and this was our time. We would spend it how we deemed best. But make no mistake about it: we weren't backing down from the personal challenge of completing our journey. If we needed some help along the way to preserve Debbie's employment, if not our own safety, so be it. Besides, our upcoming connections with loved ones would allow them to share in the joy of our recent marriage.

A long walk to the Great Falls AAA office provided maps and additional advice on routes into North Dakota. I plotted a course using the northern alternative that would land us at motels for five consecutive nights. Mileage between these motels was optimistic. We would need to average seventy-three miles per day, with one of those days approaching ninety miles. I wondered how Debbie's rear end would hold up.

Although our physical rest was beneficial, we were anxious to get back on the road. Daily, I had to remind Debbie we weren't leaving until we got clearance from the doctor's office. On Thursday morning, we went for a follow-up visit. The nurse practitioner was able to drain some of the abscess. She gave us clearance to resume our trip.

I could really relate to the nurse practitioner's assistant. She had overcome substance abuse, too. I shared with her how God had delivered me from my own personal crisis over twenty years ago. I had suffered from anorexia and bulimia, and had been addicted to alcohol. I made some poor choices—decisions I regret to this day. I was totally broken and came to a serious crossroads. On April 11, 1989, I cried out to Jesus to save me. He did—and He has. I've ridden a long road to recovery with the help of Alcoholics Anonymous, supportive Christian friends, my love for reading the Bible and praying, and the Spirit of God living inside me. Thanks be to God!

*As Lewis and Clark, along with Sacajawea, stand guard over
the Missouri River, a rainbow appears*

Re-launching

We left the doctor's office in Great Falls with a newfound energy, and
our rested bodies now agreed with our upbeat frame of mind. The
starting gate had been thrown wide open. We scurried back to the
motel, checked out, and headed for Fort Benton. Five days in Great
Falls could have translated into 200 to 300 miles, even as more than
400 miles still separated us from North Dakota. But after fifteen
straight days of riding, we were glad to have caught our breath. We
were happy to be moving again and looking forward to what lay
ahead—and the flatter the better. With training now officially over,
it was time to increase the pace.

With plenty of expendable energy and enthusiasm, our late start
was irrelevant. We departed town on a bike path along the banks of
the Missouri River, treated to the loud sound of rushing water from
which our haven of the past several days took its name. We circum-
vented the large rectangular footprint of the Malmstrom Air Force
Base on the eastern outskirts of town. Soon, we returned to lengthy
vistas over sparse farmland and barren plains. A lone, distant
mountain range met the partially cloudy sky, as if waving good-bye
from the Rocky Mountain West. We enjoyed a fifty-five-mile day
on isolated roads and arrived in Fort Benton, the self-proclaimed
birthplace of Montana.

Fort Benton was a charming place, despite its population of only 1,500 residents. A series of plaques and statues on the waterfront commemorate the town's history, which draws from the early settling of the West on the Missouri River. In the 1800s, the falls located upriver established the town as a destination for steamboats from the Mississippi. The downtown building façades looked Wild West, as if from a 1960s Hollywood set.

Fort Benton, Montana

A challenging day of riding followed our trip back in time at Fort Benton. Crosswinds, rumble strips, and oversized vehicles commanded our attention until we arrived in Havre late in the day. It was a stressful day of riding—one of those days when you struggle for every mile. As air from the unusual wind patterns circulated through the vent holes in our helmets, a unique whistling sound put us on alert. Large vehicles broke the strong crosswinds, only to create a challenging draft of their own, buffeting our heavy loads to and fro. Until one rides in these conditions, it is difficult to understand the feeling of vulnerability and lack of control, especially when trying to steer a heavy load clear of

Pronghorn "antelope"

rumble strips that could topple or damage the bike. An occasional riding miscalculation or loss of control would quickly result in one's tires dipping into the rumble strip, launching a pounding sensation from the tire to the forearms and shoulders, and on up to the rattle of unclenched teeth. Despite threatening skies and a hazardous road, we made it to the Hi-Line, US Route 2 running east-west across the top of Montana.

Riding the Hi-Line

Shortly after leaving Havre on a beautifully warm and sunny day with miles of open road awaiting us, we did not suspect trouble ahead. A few miles down the road, however, Debbie's rear set of panniers came crashing to the pavement. Unfazed, Debbie kept right on pedaling.

"Stop!" I yelled, not once, but twice.

Our second mechanical test of the trip stared defiantly at us. A screw holding Debbie's rear rack onto the bicycle frame had come off. Two pinholes appeared in one of her panniers, but that was the least of our concerns. Although sliding panniers along asphalt is never advisable, a little duct tape would patch those holes nicely. The more challenging issue was reattaching the rack. It needed to be secure due to the heavy load Debbie was carrying. So, there we were, out in the middle of nowhere, left to our own devices. Staving off any feelings of panic, we began searching the area for the escaped screw.

A nearby resident stopped to lend a hand and then went to retrieve some tools and screws from his garage. While he was gone, I found a matching spare screw on my bicycle. Seemed my rack had an extra screw, which was just what we needed to affix Debbie's rack back onto the frame. Moments later, when our Good Samaritan returned, we thanked him for his kindness while hiding any smug looks that might have suggested we knew what we were doing. As if repairing the problem were not uplifting enough, we found the screw that had flown off Debbie's rack. With our spare screw now in hand and our confidence bolstered, we resumed our ride.

The Hi-Line of eastern Montana

Riding the Hi-Line, US Route 2 in eastern Montana, was incredible. I asked Debbie, "How do you describe this to someone who hasn't been here?" There it was in front of us, a solitary road with solitude, a periodic sighting of a parallel rail line its only companion along miles and miles of open road, farther than the eye could see. A deep blue sky with a smattering of small, happy, white clouds dancing on the horizon in another land far, far away covered beautiful plains stretching to infinity on either side. With my special companion, my bride, with me, solitude would not mean a lonely day.

Rail line: companion of the Hi-Line

The daily task was simple: make it to the next motel, seventy miles of open road on the high plain. Lunch awaited at a ghost town along the way. There were no homes or other buildings, and no trees— only grass and some intermittent, soft golden, larger-than-life wheat fields. The comfort of dry, 90-degree heat, a gentle tailwind, little traffic, and virtually no hills except for the inconspicuous decline hundreds of miles in advance of the Dakotas promised stress-free pedaling. Meanwhile, the Continental Divide faded as a distant memory hundreds of miles in the rearview mirror. Thousands of easy and steady pedal strokes awaited on a road so straight that its architect no doubt used a straightedge to design it. This was my idea of a cross-country bicycle ride. The well-paved road was all ours on a smooth-sailing journey whose end gratefully was not in sight, as our eyes clearly saw.

Ahead, in the middle of our nowhere, stood the only erect structure in miles, other than an occasional road sign. An historical

The high prairie of eastern Montana

marker, entitled "Buffalo Country," described the demise of those nearly extinct creatures that roamed this region by the thousands a century or more ago. The regrettable history of the magnificent high plain is taught to passersby, evoking a moment or two of silence to grieve the savagery and greed of our ancestors, causing us to wonder about a time gone by and what might have been.

Periodic reminders of life, like a salute from an occasional passing motorist or honorary toots from a freight train, passed us by. How did such a well-paved road come to be where there are no people? Although some may call this area desolate, partly for this reason I would call it a touring cyclist's paradise.

In the distance appeared a water tower forewarning of civilization ahead. I asked Debbie, "How far away do you think that water tower is?" She responded, "Two miles?"

Five miles later, we had learned yet another lesson of time and space on the mystifying high plain when we finally arrived at a small

The vast and expansive open road

community at the base of the tower whose size had grown steadily for the last twenty-five minutes. You do not see this back East!

In the days and weeks ahead, we experienced many long stretches of road and adjacent plains, but nowhere as grand and sparsely populated as eastern Montana. The views were no longer to infinity. The width and depth of the vast expanses began to shrink. As the Midwest arrived, trees sprang up, rivers and streams emerged, and even people appeared. Cropping up yet farther east were homes, farms, and grid-like road systems with street names like 2000N and 1100W, where the corn stalks inhibited the visibility of crisscrossing traffic. Somehow, it was not quite the same. Words do it little justice. Real comprehension only comes from being there.

Miles east sat an empty condominium surrounded by endless hubbub, busy people conducting daily life in the suburbs of Boston—the crisscrossing of stop-and-go traffic commuting to work, working parents shuffling their children between daycare and soccer, and freight trucks speeding toward delivery deadlines. The honking horns, screeching tires, vile looks, and obscene gestures of irate motorists on the highway treadmill were a distant memory, as were work deadlines and the pressure to perform. Here in eastern Montana—this was the beautiful and carefree existence we had dreamed about. Or was it?

Several roadside signs on the Hi-Line encouraged youth to avoid meth and alcohol. Some of the exhibits showcased grisly wreckage reclaimed from the junkyard. Given the warnings of people in Great Falls several days earlier about an area with a bad reputation for alcoholism and crime, we were already cautious and wondering what we might encounter. Even a portending weather forecast for potentially violent thunderstorms raised caution on this day. In one small town, a Native American woman, noticing our touring bicycles, asked about our itinerary. Citing youth gang activity, she had specific recommendations about where not to stay or tarry. In a town farther down the road, another individual reported three murders in the next town in the past week.

I really didn't like the notion of traveling through high crime zones, if indeed we were about to, especially with Debbie along. As a brand-new husband, I felt a compulsion to protect Debbie from harm. When touring by bicycle, we came to learn we were at the mercy of those around us. I'm convinced 99.9% of the people we encountered meant us no harm. To the contrary, most wanted to help us. But just as when you walk down a dark alley in a city at night, your own personal well-being can be at higher risk. And due to the tendency for bad men to exploit good women, it stands to reason that women and those who seek to protect them are at even higher risk. But it was also clear we had chosen a path we couldn't turn back from now. So, I said another prayer and just kept pedaling.

> I wasn't very concerned about traveling along the Hi-Line in eastern Montana, despite what people had told us about the area. Tim is much more cautious than I am. For me, it just added to the thrill of our adventure. Deep down, I knew why he was concerned. But I also knew God would protect us.

As we approached the apparent epicenter, disheveled vehicles sped by. Gone were the friendly gestures and encouraging toots. A feeling of depression and oppression crept in, belying the lovely landscapes and warm, welcoming weather. A junkyard accompanied our ride into town. A string of loosely connected wooden doors formed a makeshift façade with more missing teeth than not, about as incapable of hiding the wreckage within as tight jeans on an overweight plumber checking beneath the kitchen sink. Ugliness spilled out all around—there was simply no hiding it. A horse sauntered among the beat-up cars much like the stray dogs we saw milling about the streets. Inside a convenience store, a stone-faced woman sat lifeless in front of a gambling machine, punching her next ticket to misery. Meanwhile, the cashier kept ringing up beer sales. Abandoned buildings marred with graffiti and boarded-up churches were ominous signs that all was not well. If ever there was a place to post cards for TheHopeLine, this was it. Yet, one proprietor suggested the people were so apathetic they probably wouldn't call. It broke our hearts.

The irony was as baffling and monumental as the surrounding plains themselves. In an area physically so beautiful, so pristine, and so unbridled, how could it be, as one person described, "not a very happy area, with a lot of teen suicide and domestic abuse," or as another said, "just a bad place"? One can't help but ask, "Who or what is to blame?" But then again, the human condition fails to measure up wherever one looks, even within our own beings. The caution of our inner senses and our own timetable overruled the burning desire to investigate further. We left the area as we had entered it: no sightseeing, no pictures, no lengthy conversations with locals, and no wasting time.

Our bittersweet departure from Montana came with an incident reminiscent of day one on the Hi-Line, an illustration of how our bicycle tour redefined what was of value. We were cycling alongside the railroad tracks on a very hot day when Debbie suddenly lost the bite valve to her Camelbak. A Camelbak is a hydration system that stores and dispenses cold liquids from an insulated bladder. The bite valve acts as a nipple to regulate the flow of the fluid and keep it within the bladder when not in use. Debbie had taken a drink and the valve came loose and blew away. The water began pouring out—all over her. Without the nipple, her Camelbak, which had been an invaluable tool to sustain her hydration in these remote regions, became useless.

An item worth only a few dollars had instantly become priceless. The bite valve is a specialty part. Who knew where the next Camelbak dealer was? The heat intensified as we combed the area for at least a half hour in search of the wayward valve. We tried reconstructing the mishap, to no avail. Finally, we gave it up for lost. Just as we resumed our ride, Debbie miraculously spotted the elusive nipple in some tall grass. Just as the missing rack screw had reemerged days earlier, the nipple mysteriously reappeared as well.

As much as the seediness of humanity, incidents like these reminded us of our vulnerability. If it isn't the big things, seemingly inconsequential things can impede progress. Why and when they happen, only God knows. On this particular occasion, we resumed travel in a remote area knowing Debbie had a good supply of water capable of sustaining her into more populous regions. Details can be very important.

We spotted one last white roadside cross as we left Montana, yet another solemn reminder of the hazards of the road and the power of the internal combustion engine. Thirteen days and over 600 miles later, we had crossed a state with breathtaking beauty and expansiveness. We were about to enter another.

8. Tornado Alley

As we neared the North Dakota border, there stood an oil rig with its constant circular motion, its squeaky, massive arm bobbing up and down, the whole structure a misfit of the beautiful landscape of eastern Montana. We were about to see many more. Once across the border in North Dakota, the pace of traffic soon increased. Large oil industry vehicles rumbled by, governed more by work schedules and paychecks than our safety. The Hi-Line had indeed become an industrial work zone, and the staff apparently clocked out at sundown. Montana had been a time zone unto itself. We had now entered the central time zone, with plenty of daylight for early evening oil operations.

Reunion

We arrived in Williston in time for supper. After a phone call to Laurie and a visit to an ATM, we were back on the road prepared to rendezvous with our hosts somewhere on Route 2 East. Sure enough, after several miles, a shiny red pickup pulled a U-turn and joined us by the side of the road.

> Seeing Laurie again after all these years was so emotional. We shared the same profession and have known one another for many years since our days in Colorado. Since we were unable to attend each other's wedding, this was also a chance to introduce our Tims.

After introductions and some brief conversation, we loaded the panniers and bicycles into the back of the pickup. Laurie's husband, Tim, immediately indulged us with a tour of the area's oil rigs and farmland. The change in speed from bicycle travel was startling. In just over three weeks, our bodies had forgotten what travel in a motorized vehicle was like. After an ice cream treat during the

113

10:30 sunset, Tim drove us to their cattle ranch in Powers Lake, where we spent the next two nights.

After the long daily mileage of the past week, we welcomed a rest day. We witnessed up close the demands, as well as the alluring lifestyle, of farming in a small community. Work responsibilities wrestle for Tim and Laurie's time, particularly on a seasonal basis. As ranchers, they shoulder significant operational and financial risks. Among the rewards for this responsibility is living in a beautiful land with a caring and close-knit community at hand. The wholesome lifestyle reminded me of the area in Maine where I grew up.

On our second evening in North Dakota, Debbie and I enjoyed another dazzling sunset. Because of the flat topography and lack of trees, the North Dakota sky was Montana-sized and, therefore, offered lengthy and fabulous sunsets. We saw plenty of orange sky. Massive fields brimming with bountiful crops met the horizon, which in the western portion of the state was dotted with oil rigs. At dusk and into the twilight, flickers of infinite flame appeared with each rig, creating a unique and ironic beauty where man and nature delightfully coexisted. Tim and Laurie topped off their warm hospitality with a bonfire overlooking their beautiful and spacious property.

Sunset in Powers Lake, North Dakota

We appreciated them opening up their home and lives to us.

The following day, Laurie transported us out of the oil-producing area to Minot. Debbie and Laurie celebrated their reunion with a trip to Starbucks while I purchased supplies at Walmart. We filled Laurie's truck with gas and prepared for departure. The process reminded me of that feeling in Oregon when Debbie's cousin Jim helped us launch our tour. It would be just the two of us again, along with our gear. As I loaded our panniers on our bicycles, I was feeling like I had just graduated from high school and was leaving home for college—that same feeling of anxiety and adventure swept over me. But it was not as strong as day one's—we were more experienced now. We knew what to expect and how to cope. And we knew one another better. Nevertheless, it was another good-bye.

> The break was great. I loved seeing Laurie in her North Dakota surroundings. I never thought I would have this opportunity. As we got ready to depart, I wondered whether I would ever see her again. She has been such a good and supportive friend over the years, but we live so far apart.
>
> It was also wonderful to see a female friend. Tim and I had been together since the start of our trip. Sometimes, women just need time with women. Nevertheless, I was also excited about getting back on the road and being alone again with Tim. I could hardly wait to get rolling.

Accelerating the Pace

Midway through our sixty-mile trip to Rugby, we encountered what I have come to know as the "downer at Towner"—Towner, North Dakota, that is. Route 2 in this region was a divided four-lane highway, but construction reduced the eastbound travel to only one lane, the lane closest to the shoulder. Paying close attention to the trailing traffic was important to our well-being. The shoulder was narrow and shared space with another nasty rumble strip. As I focused on steering clear of traffic, I began to pull away from Debbie. Eventually, I stopped and looked back. Debbie was no longer in sight.

Normally, I would just go back to find her. But I couldn't with these road conditions.

So, I decided to call Debbie on my cell phone. She was in tears. I immediately thought the worst. *Has she fallen? Has she hurt herself? Did her bicycle break down? What has happened?* Between her sniffles, I learned one of the bungee cords holding gear onto her rear rack had come loose and gotten caught in the spokes. *Oh, no!* I thought. *She must have broken some spokes.* I then learned her sandal had fallen off the bike into the roadside brush somewhere in the last however-many miles. She had unsuccessfully hunted for it. I was frankly relieved that she and her bicycle were still roadworthy, but also somewhat miffed she would get so upset at something so harmless. After all, she wasn't hurt and we still had transportation home. Nevertheless, she was overwhelmed with sadness. If it weren't for the construction, we would have hunted for the shoe until we found it. But under the circumstances, and with an ominous sky overhead, we decided to move on.

> I loved those sandals. They were my favorite shoes. I was mad at myself. I knew I should have packed them in the pannier. We would need to purchase another pair of street shoes—and we wouldn't find a pair like that in a town this size.
>
> Later in the motel room, I was faced with discarding the other one. It was useless without its mate—it merely added extra weight. Throwing it away was like pouring more salt into the wound.

As we continued to ride, the sky became darker and darker, completely overcast with black, billowy clouds threatening to deluge us. Thankfully, we arrived in Rugby before the skies opened up. That evening, we avoided tumultuous thunderstorms. For hours, lightning flashed and thunder crashed. But we were under the cover of our motel, enjoying another special night as newlyweds. The next morning, our amazing stretch of dry and warm riding weather would continue.

Rugby, North Dakota, claims the distinction of being the geographical center of North America. From looking at our maps, however, we were not convinced we had hit our midpoint yet. We decided to leave the Hi-Line on the next day due to flooding east of Rugby. This would force us to rely on other road maps. The turn-by-turn Adventure Cycling maps and the beautiful places to which they'd brought us would be set aside for a few days.

We were in good riding shape now, and it was time to take advantage. Thus far, we had averaged sixty-four miles a day. We weren't sure how many miles remained in our trip, but we estimated that eighty-five miles a day would enable a timely arrival at the Atlantic Ocean. Any rest days would either increase the required daily average or reduce the days available for Debbie to prepare for the beginning of school.

We also had the option of shortening our route or having people shuttle us forward. The thought of not finishing at the Atlantic repulsed us. It would feel like we had not reached our goal, despite bicycling over 3,000 miles to go directly to our home. So, as August and our trip midpoint simultaneously approached, it was beginning to look like we would not make it to the Atlantic in time for Debbie's return to school. Laurie's shuttle service to Minot had eliminated 125 miles of our trip, but more would be required. Willing friends and relatives lay ahead. In the meantime, we knew we had more daily mileage within us. The length of day was still ample, and we were now in the right place to crank out the miles. The next two days, with a favorable wind, we rode over ninety miles each day through the heart of North Dakota. It felt wonderful—we were in the groove.

This was wheat country with miles and miles of flat land, well-paved roads, and little traffic. The low stress level also promoted longer days. True to advanced billing, North Dakota was a friendly state with beautiful farmland gracing our journey. Even the animals were friendly. At one impromptu rest stop on the side of the road, a herd of cattle gathered in an adjacent field. A pen of vast acreage couldn't contain their curiosity as they congregated fence-side to investigate our world. They were most entertaining on a hot afternoon in the flatland.

Curious cows

In the eastern portion of the state, another beautiful sunset took center stage. The sunlight skidded across the pavement, creating a reflective sheen of deep yellow as if Highway 200 had become a mirror. The North Dakota sunsets added an exclamation point to the beauty of each day and acted as lasting reminders of how much God had blessed our lives.

We arrived at a campground within the town limits of Mayville, North Dakota, just after sunset. We hadn't camped since Idaho and weren't really planning to this evening. A local wedding party had claimed all motel rooms, so we began pitching our tent for the evening. Before we had placed our stakes, a strong wind arose, lifted the tent, and carried it like a tumbleweed toward the adjacent river. After bicycling ninety-three miles, sprinting after a runaway tent while my wife laughed was not my idea of getting the evening off to a good start. A lapse in the strong gale allowed me to retrieve our

Debbie approaching Mayville, North Dakota

bedroom. A camping neighbor then came by to alert us of tornado warnings. He pointed us to the campground's concrete bathroom in the event of wild weather. In time, the wind abated, and we were able to pitch our tent and catch some sleep.

Early the next morning, the joyful chirping of birds awakened us. It would have been a most delightful way to start the morning had it not been for the 191 miles of cycling in the prior two days, and bodies crying out for more rest. But Debbie was able to enjoy the fresh fragrance and beautiful sights of an adjacent municipal flower garden. And our early wake-up call facilitated a timely arrival at a Sunday church service just up the road.

Passing through North Dakota introduced a major change in weather patterns. We had migrated from a region with typically arid conditions to one where humidity predominates. One hundred degrees in an arid climate is more comfortable than 100 degrees in a humid climate. In fact, 100 arid degrees may even feel better than 90 humid degrees. The humidity also brings a higher risk of thunderstorms and tornados. While tornado activity is typically more prevalent in the spring, it also occurs in the dead of summer. Tornado activity is particularly concerning for bicycle tourists in the Midwest because there is no protection, either on the bicycle or in the region's vast expanses of farmland. Checking The Weather Channel immediately became part of the daily routine.

Celebrity Status?

As we rolled across the Red River at Fargo into Minnesota, the character of the landscape changed almost immediately. The farmland was not as expansive, although tracts were still large. We saw more trees, houses, roads, and lakes. When a state boasts 10,000 lakes, I suppose there are only so many places to put them. Their water merely accentuated the beautiful scenery that we had become accustomed to seeing. Large geese with sensitive ears and impressive wingspans jumped us on several occasions as they arose honking from the reeds, ramping up to a graceful flight, and falling quickly into formation. Whereas the rural and wholesome character of

North Dakota reminded me of that of my hometown, the Minnesota landscape was similar to that of Maine, albeit on a grander scale. The little-traveled, low-speed farm roads offered more tranquility than we had enjoyed on our trip to date.

Minnesota

While Tim spent much of his break time navigating, I read from a daily devotional booklet in the transparent map case on the top of my handle-bar bag. I found incredible peace by talking to God while riding along. I would talk and sing until on the verge of tears. Sometimes, I had a "song of the day," usually with a spiritual flavor, which would play repeatedly in my mind as the miles passed by. What an unexpected blessing to have open-ended quiet time with God—and right in the midst of His beautiful creation!

We soon realized Minnesotans had a high regard for bicycle tourists. We had one person want to shake our hands, another inter-cept us on the road to chat and offer us a bed in his house, a third stop by a rest area to see if we had missed a turn, and others just inquiring and being friendly. At the visitor center in Bowlus, which acted as a hub for recreational activities on nearby converted rail trails, we learned of Minnesota's bicycle route system. A woman at the Dairy Queen in Royalton was thrilled to speak with us. In her words: "You've made my day!" Her daughter was an avid cyclist who had trained with Lance Armstrong's team and done some long-distance touring of her own.

With this heightened attention to our endeavor, Debbie and I began to feel like rock stars. We really weren't sure what the fuss was about, but the genuine warmth and hospitality was most welcoming. Soon enough, Uncle Chuck and Aunt Melinda, and their daughters,

Facing page: Leaving North Dakota

Jennifer and Jaime, continued this treatment. Reconnecting with them provided a much needed break. Chuck and Melinda went out of their way by meeting us in Foreston and transporting us to their cabin north of Minneapolis. I slept in while Debbie went kayaking with Chuck. Debbie's energy level never ceases to amaze me.

Chuck and Melinda had taken a special interest in our trip from its inception with regular comments on our blog. In fact, the support of all family and friends, plus some strangers, in the form of blog comments made us feel like we were not alone. Because our daily routine was so focused on making trip progress, viewing blog comments and e-mail became a highly anticipated daily event, akin to checking the mailbox to see what treasures the mail carrier had left.

For our second night with Chuck and Melinda, they drove us south to their daughter Jennifer's home in Red Wing, Minnesota, stopping at an outdoor recreation store on the way where we purchased some supplies. A special additional stop at a Dairy Queen demonstrated they understood us well, as did their idea for the following day, when they brought us to the National Eagle Center on the banks of the Mississippi River in Wabasha, Minnesota. Given the significance the eagle has played in our lives, it isn't difficult to see why such a visit would be so meaningful to us. The center had live eagles and plenty of information about our nation's symbol.

Our sights were beginning to focus on the Atlantic Ocean. Chuck and Melinda's special care provided rest and recovery. We appreci-

ated being able to share our unique experience with them. Their shuttle service allowed us to bypass metropolitan Minneapolis and saved us two days of riding time, knocking another 155 miles off our route.

On the next day, we resumed bicycling south along the Mississippi River. After only forty miles, we rendezvoused

Supportive family

with a long-time friend of mine named Mike Porter. Mike, his wife, Anne, and their two teenage sons lived in Wisconsin, just across the river. Mike insisted on taking us to their lovely cabin a few hours east on the Wisconsin River for an evening.

The Porters' cabin was indeed a wonderful place, despite the unusual onslaught of mosquitoes upon our arrival. The company was even better than the facility. Although I'd met Mike in high school through our shared passion for competitive chess, and although Mike had chosen a serious profession as a pathologist, he is undoubtedly one of the funnier, more entertaining people I know. The chess tournaments we'd played in together since high school had produced many fond and meaningful memories.

The two evenings that we spent with Mike and his family were more than just a time to reminisce. We discovered and celebrated where life had brought us. Debbie was even able to fit in some exercise on her "day off," kayaking on the Wisconsin River with Mike and Anne's son Ryan.

As always, it was great to share some laughs with Mike. However, this time, Debbie had the last laugh. Since she had developed an ache in one of her feet during our travels, Doctor Mike agreed to examine it. The foot wasn't very sore, but it was clearly swollen. He gently poked and prodded while asking, "Does this hurt?" After several of his inquiries, Debbie jumped and exclaimed, "Ouch!" After a moment, she laughed, exposing her exaggerated response. Anne laughed and said, "That's just like something Michael would have pulled." The rest of us, especially the good doctor himself, burst into laughter.

I was glad the Porters were able to meet and spend some time with Debbie before Mike returned us downstream of our originally intended route. We were again overwhelmed with

Dr. Mike, the comedic ringleader!

Midwestern hospitality, and most grateful. When Mike dropped us in Cascade, Iowa, eliminating yet another 155 miles from our journey, Debbie and I knew our next time with family and friends would be at the end of our trip. We also knew we had only about twenty days to complete it. And we hadn't yet chosen how and where to end it.

Our return trip to the open road in Mike's pickup was lively. We traveled through a long, continuous thunderstorm with copious rainfall and lightning. It was hard to imagine riding bicycles with those violent bolts of electricity looking for something—or someone—to fry. And visibility would have been a big problem. This was the type of storm you waited out underneath an overpass. I was just glad we didn't need to. Before parting ways with Mike, we shared a lunch at the local Subway. Again, as if timed from On High, the skies were clear when we began pedaling.

Corn and Soybeans

On this day, we would continue our southward trek. We had long since decided to skirt the Great Lakes rather than ferry across them. We wanted to explore more states. So, we needed to drop down farther to avoid Lake Michigan and the busy metropolitan Chicago area. Even though north-south travel seemed counterproductive, it was necessary to stay on track.

When we met Jim—a Nashville, Tennessee, car salesman who was bicycling solo east-to-west with his trailer in tow—we were reminded of two blessings. First, Jim's bicycle had experienced all sorts of mechanical problems. Other than a loose rack screw and one flat tire, we'd had none. We knew people were praying for our safety and our time together, so we were grateful. The second issue was more troubling: Jim was alone. Despite being pressed for time, we chatted at length with him. He needed it. We could tell he was lonely. Nonetheless, Jim deserved a lot of credit. He was letting neither his solitude nor his mechanical issues get in the way of pursuing his dream.

Debbie and I had tried to live our single lives with that same determination. Had it not been for God's provision, we would have been in Jim's shoes—yet again. We didn't relish his experience one bit, as we had already been there. I suppose the only thing worse than journeying solo would be sharing the journey with the wrong person. You can't stop living life waiting for perfect conditions, and Jim had obviously embraced that. But when you are delivered from the plague of loneliness, you don't want to go back. And neither would you wish it upon anyone else. Debbie and I could not have conceived of venturing cross-country without one another. Doing it alone could not possibly have measured up to sharing the experience with one another. Although we were newly married, we assumed the same to be true for life itself.

After wishing Jim well and parting ways, we continued on, enjoying the impressive landscape of eastern Iowa. Vast acreages of corn and soybeans promised a teeming harvest. Gone were most of the lush wheat fields of our past travels. Instead, corn was the crop of choice, systematically climbing up and down the rolling hills like an escalator. From higher ground, this labyrinth of huge fields, sprinkled with a dash of farm buildings, was a beautiful master-piece testifying to the fertility, industriousness, and abundant riches of America's heartland. We didn't expect the hills. Coupled with a stiff cross breeze, they challenged us. Our ride became reminiscent of Idaho weeks earlier, when our destination outlasted not only a fabulous sunset over magnificent rolling fields, but also some dusk

Eastern Iowa

riding with headlamps. Pesky bugs accompanied the darkness, further frustrating our efforts. Our will had been broken. We would reach Muscatine, Iowa, and the banks of the Mississippi tomorrow.

We stayed the evening at a small inexpensive motel in Wilton. In the morning, we listened to an ominous weather forecast on the television. The friendly chambermaid substantiated my concerns with her own forecast. When she used the term "tornado alley," my concerns kicked up a notch. Outside, at ten o'clock in the morning, the sky was dark. "We're not leaving until the weather clears," I said.

Debbie wasn't happy. We were already behind schedule and it was time to make up for lost ground. But I didn't care. We weren't going to venture out when we knew there was a high probability of precipitation accompanied by an electrical storm—with an outside chance of encountering high winds or even a tornado. The rumbling in the distance overshadowed the grumbling within, strengthening my argument and my resolve.

> We could have been stuck in that motel room for hours. It was barely raining outside—just some cloud cover. Why did we bring raingear if we weren't going to use it?
>
> Tim will analyze things until the cows come home. He calculates decisions carefully—must be his chess training. I just like to go with the flow. Sometimes, I wish he would just loosen up a bit. But I do like the fact he is concerned about me and thinks things through.

I really didn't like the idea of bicycling across the Plains with the possibility of severe weather. Maybe the fear of the unknown was spooking me. Or maybe I had simply watched too many storm chasers on television. I have spent most of my life in Maine, where severe weather takes the form of minus-35-degree temperatures, three-foot blizzards, or spring flooding. Sure, we had thunderstorms in the summer, but tornados? Maybe a couple a year, but certainly not on the Midwest scale reported on the national news.

I had also come to realize that Debbie did not have a good appreciation for danger—any danger. Perhaps that was part of my calling in life—to keep her safe. Heaven only knows she's gotten herself into enough predicaments over the years. She never saw a thrill she didn't want to pursue. Whether skiing, flying, climbing, or water sports, she's the first one in line. But the fact of the matter is I would not be on this trip without her. Having her spirit of adventure in my life enhances it, as uncomfortable as it sometimes makes me feel.

Another hour later, the skies had started to clear. We had to cross the Plains sometime and, given Debbie's schedule, we didn't have time for extended stops. Besides, this 1960s vintage strip motel wasn't going to provide much protection if severe weather struck. So, we headed out and reached the Mississippi in short order.

We had confronted the Mississippi River in several locations. We crossed its headwaters in Minnesota, where the mighty Mississippi was anything but. While picturesque from that sighting, one could not have imagined how it could grow so much deeper and wider miles to the south. On the Minnesota and Wisconsin border, we caught a glimpse of this scale where the river had grown to perhaps four times wider. The comparatively larger width provided attractive views of both the river and its Wisconsin shoreline.

We had crossed the river in vehicles with Chuck and Melinda, and Mike, but here at Muscatine, Iowa, we would finally cross it by bicycle, and cross it for good. The Mississippi seemed like a significant landmark on a cross-country ride. We were pleased it was behind us and we were heading due east, toward home.

Crossing the Mississippi

Cornfield east of the Mississippi

We had entered Illinois, the Land of Lincoln. The weather cleared into a beautiful, albeit hot and humid, day with another adverse wind battling us. Several miles of climbing lifted us out of the Mississippi River valley and onto a plateau of magnificent and gargantuan cornfields. I really didn't know what to expect from Illinois, but I certainly didn't expect this. Abundance stared at us from all directions. And the amount of climbing in each of the last two days came as a surprise, exceeding that of any day since we'd left the Rockies. We had just surpassed 2,000 miles for our trip and were over halfway home. Despite the elements and the late start, we were determined. We again rode a splendid sunset into the dusk, piling up ninety miles in one of our strongest days of riding yet. A pizza deliveryman met us by coincidence upon arrival at our motel in Kewanee. We sent him back for supper and enjoyed a restful evening inside the comfort of our motel room.

The next day, August 10, was a sultry day, with temperatures well into the 90s. Another atypical wind pattern impeded our progress. It wasn't supposed to happen like this, as the prevailing west-to-east wind should have been our ally throughout the Plains. But it didn't matter. We were prepared for days like this now. Soaking up this much sun after thirty years behind a desk was glorious. And we had the routine down. Sleep, eat, drink, clean, plan, and document—then do it all over again the next day. And, of course, throw in quite a bit of pedaling between sleeping and cleaning. Although it sounds simple, a disciplined approach in adhering to these principles was critical to pleasure, if not survival, on the road. We learned this, sometimes the hard way, as part of our on-the-job training in the first two weeks of our tour. In fact, our ritual had become much like a job, but not one that tethered us to a desk or confined us to a building. We were pleased with this job.

Illinois sunset

I learned a lot about nutrition and exercise because of the eating disorders I suffered from earlier in life. Healthy eating is now an important part of my life.

It was hard to consume enough calories to sustain energy throughout the day. Each of us lost weight despite eating large portions at all meals. A healthy breakfast of pancakes, eggs, oatmeal, and toast or muffins helped launch us for the day. Subway restaurants were great lunch stops for nutrition and convenience. Pizza and pasta were common staples in the evening. We supplemented our meals with bananas, nuts, and energy bars while riding, and ice cream several nights a week.

Drinking plenty of fluids was particularly important in this heat and humidity. Each of us carried a seventy-ounce Camelbak and three twenty-ounce water bottles. Even after tanking up on orange juice at breakfast, we typically consumed all of this fluid—and the same amount once again after refills—before the day was out. In addition, we would guzzle a thirty-two-ounce energy drink or a large fountain soda at a convenience store or restaurant. In the evening, we were typically thirsty and continued to ingest liquids. It seemed we couldn't get enough.

Debbie had the cleaning and water bottle duties of our daily routine down to a science. While she laundered the cycling apparel and managed the fluids, I charged the electronic devices, downloaded photos, tended to the blog, and planned the next day's itinerary. Occasionally, we swapped duties.

At our mid-afternoon lunch stop at a Subway in Henry, Illinois, we met a sixty-five-year-old farmer named Dale who continued to feed my fixation on Midwestern weather. Dale farmed 1,500 acres of corn and soybean in the area, so weather was an important consideration to his livelihood. He was a kind gentleman who took an interest in our well-being.

Tornados had shredded two of Dale's outbuildings recently. We already knew winds were prevalent in this area because of the windmills we saw planted amongst the corn. He explained how hot, humid days like this one could bring tumultuous weather toward evening. He surmised we had a couple more hours of worry-free riding, but storm clouds could develop thereafter.

I started thinking more about his outbuildings as well as some blemishes we had seen in the fields. *Isn't it probable there are many more tornados than we hear about?* I thought. *After all, if no one is around, or if only a small number of people are affected, would the news or reporting services cover them? And given the long distances between towns, aren't there high odds of twisters dropping down in between, never to be seen by man?* I was uneasy. Even on a muggy day in Maine, a thunderstorm is most likely to strike at around four thirty in the afternoon.

Dale also cautioned us about poor visibility due to the high corn stalks. He said vehicles would often speed through intersections because there was so little traffic in these fields, regardless of whether a stop sign was present. In worst-case scenarios, fatalities had occurred. In fact, one had happened recently on the road we had just traveled. It was easy to believe people would assume no one was coming in the other direction. We hadn't seen anyone in the fields since we'd entered the state—no workers or machinery. There was plenty of life in those fields, but it was all plant life. Where were all the people? Perhaps it was just too hot to be outside, or perhaps there was no need this time of year. We thanked Dale for his information, said our good-byes, and resumed our travel, realizing it was getting later by the moment.

As we squiggled our way through the curvy and hilly Illinois River valley, we saw the house, just as Dale had described. A tornado had destroyed it and rebuilding efforts were underway. The adjacent homes were completely unscathed. *Interesting*, I thought. *What would we do out here if a tornado haphazardly visited us?* Once we had climbed out of the valley, there was no shelter—only corn stalks and crisscrossing roads. I wondered about the warning signs.

We pedaled on. I had been scanning the sky very attentively since our meal. When we left, it was blue and beautiful. Now, however, some dark clouds had formed, seemingly out of nowhere. The clouds were not overhead, but to our sides to the north and south, and behind us to the west. They seemed harmless at the moment. But as time went on, they got larger, ever so slowly, but growing nonetheless. It began to feel like I was watching a sinister form of time-lapse photography, which would have been rather fascinating if we weren't potentially in harm's way. It was as if the clouds behind us, those to the west, were chasing us. I had a bad feeling. We were out in the middle of corn country with no shelter in sight. Dark clouds were encircling us and thunderstorms—or worse—loomed. I felt helpless. All I could do was pedal faster—and I did!

Debbie was having difficulty keeping up with me. I pointed to the cloudy sky and continued at an urgent pace. It wasn't as if Toto was ready to jump out of her handlebar bag, but the same type of drama was beginning to take shape. Despite her efforts, Debbie continued to lag until she finally stopped. She was exhausted and needed a break. With dark clouds continuing to enclose us, I had little patience for a rest break now and shortened what would normally have been a longer break. The sky was still clear overhead and in front of us, but darkness was swallowing up more blue sky by the minute, right on cue with Dale's premonition.

When you are twenty miles from the closest town and there is no shelter in sight, dark clouds have an interesting way of helping you pick up the pace. We would go off course to find shelter. A motel in Streator lay ahead. Eventually, the urgency overtook Debbie. Thirst and fatigue jumped into her rear panniers—and a mad dash ensued. Several miles later, under an overcast sky, we arrived. Relieved, we booked our room and relaxed. Most motel rooms on our trip were welcome sights, but this one was a true haven. After cleaning up, we ventured back outside into the sultry evening to an adjacent Pizza Hut for supper. Cloud-to-cloud lightning lit up the sky like fireworks. We hadn't seen a show like this since July 4 in Portland. That evening, we slept deeply and wonderfully in the comfort of our climate-controlled motel room.

> Though we had picked up the pace, it was beginning to look more and more as if we would not make it back in time for the first mandatory school day. This was really beginning to nag at me.
>
> On our way out of Streator the next morning, I called my principal to understand my options. He was very understanding and gracious. He gave me enough flexibility to assuage my growing angst.

After a morning thundershower, the wind patterns had finally changed for the better. This was what we had been waiting for. The strong tailwind and flat land enabled what felt like cruise control set at twenty-plus miles an hour. We were flying with our heavy loads. It felt great and we knew we could make great time. Would this be our first day over 100 miles? It certainly appeared possible despite the late start.

A few hours into our ride, I noticed a faint flapping sound from my front tire. The farther we rode, the louder the sound became. Finally, I stopped to examine the tire. I thought another pebble might have stuck to the rubber, aided by some gummy tar melted by the oppressive heat. However, the tread was coming apart. We had ridden in such extreme heat for much of our trip, so it wasn't surprising one of our tires had begun to fail. We had a light-duty spare tire stuffed in one of the panniers, but I wasn't giving up on this one that easily. Besides, we had duct tape onboard and there were no bicycle shops for miles. So, we continued.

A detour in Cabery presented another obstacle. We took an alternate route, adding several miles to our journey. Meanwhile, the tire noise became louder and louder. By the time we arrived in Chebanse, it was time to address the problem before the tread completely let go.

We stopped for a bite to eat. I called Tern of the Wheel located just to the north, the only full-service bike shop in the area according to the Adventure Cycling map.

When I told the young man on the other end of the line we were on a cross-country ride, he immediately deferred to the shop's owner, Steve, who we later discovered was his father. When I told Steve I was calling from Chebanse, he knew right where we were. "You're probably eating at Russ and Rosie's, aren't you?" he said.

"Yes, how'd you know?" I said.

He explained that Chebanse was not a very large place and he was familiar with the area. He had four touring tires in stock, the exact model we were using. He offered to bring them to his house, which was closer to us than his bike shop. He also offered to change the tires for us in his backyard! *You're kidding*, I thought. *This is too good a deal to pass up.* So, despite a ten-mile detour, it seemed clear what we needed to do. And a total stranger who had a business to run was making it as easy as possible for us.

When we arrived at his home, we met Steve Linneman and his wife, Joan, as well as four large family dogs. Steve and Joan invited us to stay for supper. They also offered us a bed for the evening. We were impressed with their thoughtful hospitality and gladly accepted their offer. We shared some stories about our trip, discussed cycling in general, and learned more about Steve's business and Joan's occupation. Steve also gave us bicycle maintenance pointers while changing the tires. In the morning, we went to breakfast with Joan and then rode to Tern of the Wheel in Bradley to see Steve's bike shop, to thank him, and to say good-bye. Although a mechanical problem foiled our first 100-mile day, we realized life's special blessings often come about unexpectedly. We left Illinois with warm feelings of Midwesterners and four new tires on our bicycles.

Our ride into Indiana was enjoyable until we hit the state line. The road conditions immediately disintegrated. The shoulder evaporated, the pavement eroded, and truck traffic escalated. Travel had become treacherous. Rather than haphazardly continuing to design the route as we went along, the road conditions and heavier truck traffic convinced us to head south and return to the familiarity of our Adventure Cycling map routes. The diversion of the past evening was necessary, even special, but slowed our progress considerably. North-south travel would not advance us toward the Atlantic Ocean.

Travel in Indiana soon became pastoral once again. We entered the eastern time zone on another scorcher. Narrow, seldom-traveled farm roads with alphanumeric labels, like 200W and 900N, made for delightful travel. The solitude of the beautiful farmland was striking. Trees eventually emerged along the straight, narrow roadways.

Shortly after crossing a busier road, we encountered a miniature donkey farm. The cute critters pranced toward the wooden fence at

Debbie's magnetism holds sway

the sound of Debbie's voice. As the owner beckoned, neither Debbie, nor the fence between the donkeys and her, could contain her excitement any longer. She scaled the seven-foot fence, bike cleats and all, in no time flat. I remember thinking, *Wow! How'd she do that? I couldn't do that.* Once in the pen, she got up close and personal with her newfound friends.

A few more miles down the road, another friendly Hoosier beckoned us, a farming widow who invited us in for lemonade and watermelon with one of her thirty-four grandchildren. The inviting smell of the fresh watermelon in her kitchen was reminiscent of the simple pleasures of life. The conversation was warm and hospitable—lovely, really, on a hot summer's afternoon. Realizing we were bleeding valuable time away enjoying life on the road, we headed out sooner than we would have liked. Traveling with a deadline is a good motivator, but it also means swapping interesting people, places, and activities for more riding time.

We've come to appreciate that motivation is important on a long bicycle tour. Before I even suggested to Debbie that we try this adventure, I was confident she had what it took to complete a coast-to-coast journey. However, given the frenetic pace leading into this quest, the excitement of wedding and retirement celebrations, and our lack of training, it would have been understandable if we simply rode at a comfortable pace, logged as many miles as we wanted, and then found a convenient airport and went home. In fact, that was an option in the original design.

After two weeks into our expedition, we had demonstrated a strong will to continue to the East Coast. Bicycling in near 100-degree weather into a headwind and climbing nonstop up our first significant mountain pass had convinced us. However, an incident that occurred on this day in the Midwest weeks later proved Debbie had much more drive than it took.

By late afternoon, we had bicycled about sixty-five miles in brutal, humid 90-degree heat when we arrived at what I thought would be our last stop of the day. Although we had intended more miles when the day started, enough was enough. I would not expect Debbie to go any farther in this oppressive heat. She was inside the convenience store using the bathroom while I guzzled a power drink outside.

As she opened the door to reenter the sweltering heat, I was pondering which words would allow for a gracious early end to the day. She bounced outside like a Mexican jumping bean, placing her refilled water bottles into their racks with the speed and efficiency of a short-order cook. When she looked up, unbeknownst to her, I saw beads of sweat ringed around her mouth, further substantiating my intention for an early exit. Before I could say anything, she said, "Okay, let's go!" Twenty-odd miles later, we would call it a day. That is more than what it takes! How is it that God has blessed me with this energetic woman as my wife?

Toward dusk, roadside brush had become thicker, and the terrain was beginning to change. I was riding along nonchalantly when, suddenly, I heard some commotion to my right. My heart quickened. It looked like something was hung up in an electric fence. Instantly, whatever it was had skidded to about fifteen feet in front of my bicycle. Ebbing daylight made it difficult to see, but the clatter itself was enough to send a rush of

adrenaline through my body. Just as quickly, it arose from the
pavement and darted off to my left. It was a deer! Just down
the road, we spotted two more.

We again donned headlamps for a twilight ride toward a town
with motels at the end of a productive eighty-seven-mile day.
We were intent upon making progress, and camping was simply no
longer part of our formula.

We continued east in Indiana the next day, where neat, ranch-
style houses popped up around the large soybean fields. Another
day of cruising through fields in front of a friendly tailwind went
well. We ended early at Monroeville, where the town offers free
accommodations in its pavilion for cross-country cyclists. We would
attend church there the next day and forgo two social invitations
before venturing into Ohio.

Western Ohio was beautiful. Farmland again dominated, but
trees and streams added some variety to the landscape, blending in
features we were accustomed to in New England. The area's small
towns were closer together than in previous states and made services
more abundant. The friendly small town ambiance made me feel
right at home. *I could live here*, I thought.

We reached Defiance, a city of 16,000 people at the confluence
of the Maumee and Auglaize rivers. A large, black cloud hovered
overhead, presenting a sanity test we would soon fail. Our zeal
for the road, given the flat land and supportive tailwind, got the
better of our good judgment. True to the city's name, we ventured
out before allowing the storm cloud to do its thing. A half-hour
downpour—our trip's first rainfall while we were bicycling—doused
us. But you might say we deserved it! The sound of tires rolling on
wet pavement, the cool and gritty spray on our calves, the clinging
of soaked jerseys, and glasses through which we could no longer see
reminded us we had been blessed with wonderful riding weather up
until this moment.

We would follow the Maumee River for over thirty miles to
the east. Our "short," leisurely Sunday ride of sixty-seven miles

Cycling through Indiana farmland

into Napoleon was followed by ninety-four to Milan on Monday. The bicycling here was fantastic. A healthy tailwind along with moderating temperatures and humidity helped push us to what would have been our first 100-mile day if a strategically located group of motels hadn't gotten in the way. We were tempted to continue, but with darkness setting in and Cleveland just around the corner, staying there and planning for the city cycling ahead was the right thing to do.

9. Urban Travel

THE DESK CLERK AT THE SUPER 8 in Milan, Ohio, looked concerned when I asked about bicycle routes through Cleveland. She had just checked us into the motel for the evening. I had first asked about places to stay in and around Cleveland. And as if that weren't enough, she couldn't believe we would be bicycling through the heart of the city. I'm not sure I was ready for it, either. But another side of me was looking forward to the experience. How exciting would bicycling through a major city like Cleveland be?

Erie Escape

Like many of the places along our route, we had never been to Cleveland. But I have lived long enough to know there are places to avoid when traveling through urban areas by car. How much more important would route selection be when traveling with my attractive wife by bicycle? When I showed her the two routes on our bicycling maps, the clerk seemed even more concerned. She said there were some areas along the eastern shore of Lake Erie we should avoid.

Conclusions like that always cause me strife. And conclusions like that without a deeper understanding for the reasons cause me anxiety. I know cities have challenging areas, but what did she mean by "You shouldn't go there"? Why was the bicycle map cartographer sending us there, along with thousands of other innocent cyclists? When they design these routes as cycling advocates, the tourist experience is paramount. Would they really have been leading us into harm's way?

Much as I had done in Great Falls at the first glimpse of possible concerns along the Hi-Line, my primary focus for the next few days would be understanding how to travel through Cleveland and live to tell about it. Should I trust the map or the local intelligence? Among the locals, who was most credible? And since the map offered two alternatives, could the local intelligence steer us along the safer path?

Based upon the clerk's recommendation, we booked a night in one of the safer neighborhoods on the west side of Cleveland. We could assess the situation better as we got nearer and could talk to the locals. When we left Milan the next morning, these planning considerations were forefront.

The thought of going through Cleveland didn't faze me. After all, our maps were published by "Adventure" Cycling. We hadn't been through a major city since Portland, Oregon. That was well over 2,000 miles and many weeks ago. As Tim wrestled with the details, I thought, *Bring it on! Enough of these corn and soybean fields. I'm ready for some urban bicycling.*

Just five miles into our trip the next morning, we had arrived on the shoreline of Lake Erie, west of Cleveland. Our surroundings had changed for good. The seemingly endless array of corn and soybean fields was gone, replaced by a crowded road, a long stretch of suburban landscape consisting of businesses and various forms of housing, and a nearby body of deep blue water on our left that would

Cycling toward Cleveland

shadow us for days. We pedaled east along the shoreline, joining the traffic that was heading toward Cleveland on US Route 6. Some portions of this stretch featured a bike lane; some, awkwardly slanted concrete slabs; and others, constricted space for bicycling.

We stopped at a park in Bay Village where the odor of chlorine and the sounds of children's laughter and splashing from a nearby swimming pool filled the air. We received some more ambiguous advice about riding east of Cleveland.

A conversation with an experienced cyclist only served to validate my concerns. In his words, "Sure, I've heard of horror stories about bicyclists getting attacked on their bikes over there. But it doesn't stop me from riding there. That's where I've had some of my best rides." This wasn't what I wanted to hear. Nevertheless, I filed it away for future consideration, and we resumed our ride.

We reached a pleasant residential area on the outskirts of Cleveland. Youth football practice was underway at a local field. Debbie found bathroom facilities while I handed a boy a card with TheHopeLine phone number on it. This youth looked particularly troubled to me, perhaps even angry. He was quiet, withdrawn, and sitting alone away from the crowd—downright despondent. His sad countenance lingered in my mind as we prepared to continue our journey. Although I became a trained Hope Coach after our trip, I felt ill-equipped to help him—I didn't really know how to approach the situation other than to give him the card. I prayed he would make the call and vent his issues to a trained Hope Coach.

After ten straight days of bicycling, the fatigue was evident. Debbie dropped her loaded bike, along with herself, twice when trying to resume from the parking lot. It was time for a day off. I knew Debbie had mixed feelings about taking a rest day because she was so concerned about fulfilling her responsibilities at school. But our bodies needed to recover. A break would also give us an opportunity to sightsee and plan our departing route.

Soon, our motel appeared, in residential environs, far from downtown. Large attractive houses on well-kept grounds lined the boulevard. Within walking distance were restaurants, a convenience store, and a bus stop. We seemed to be in a good place, so we checked in.

We took the bus into Cleveland on the next day to check out the sights. A leisurely stroll through downtown and along the waterfront on a beautiful sunny day was therapeutic. Johnny Cash's tour bus on display near the entrance to the Rock and Roll Hall of Fame drew us. The beat of music from the 1960s took over from there, escorting us into the museum's gift shop. We also visited the Great Lakes

Science Center and Browns Stadium on the waterfront. Although we were sluggish, we were already chomping at the bit to get back on the road. It was August 18 and school was starting in thirteen days. And we were still a long way from home.

After our first night's stay in Cleveland, I had seen, and killed, a small insect on one of the pillows in our motel room. We had just seen an article in a major newspaper, as well as televised reports, about bed bug epidemics in major US cities, Cleveland among them. I'm still not sure whether I had killed a bed bug or not, but when a brownish trickle of blood oozed out, I had my suspicions. Regardless, I didn't have a good feeling. But with another night to go, I wasn't ready to sound the alarm. I decided not to tell Debbie until later. Besides, most of our gear was inside our panniers on our bicycles. And we were showering and using alcohol swabs every day. *If we really need to get out of here,* I thought, *would anywhere else around here be any better?*

Before checking out the next morning, Debbie knocked a comb off the vanity. It fell to the floor and drew our attention to a three-inch space between the vanity and the wall. An oversized, creepy-looking bug was staring us in the face. Its body was at least two inches long and its folded up legs longer yet. It was already dead, thank goodness. But this incident prompted me to get housekeeping. My curiosity about the identity of my kill from the day before was beginning to get the better of me.

The chambermaid was just across the hall and, sensing our alarm, immediately agreed to come into our room. I wanted her to see this firsthand—and I wanted to see her reaction. Upon seeing the gigantic insect, she appeared disgusted. She quickly and quietly removed it from the room. I knew she was in an awkward position, but I wanted to know more.

"Is it typical to find bugs in these rooms?" I asked.

She didn't respond. I knew her silence was more than just the language barrier between us. Her reaction and her silence told me more than I wanted to hear. With a speedy checkout now in order, Debbie and I traded one dilemma for another.

I couldn't believe the size of the bug. When Tim told me about the other suspicious bug he had killed the day before, I couldn't get back on the road fast enough. Our room had felt so comfortable and inviting—until now.

Finding relief in the open air pushed us headlong into our next adventure. Yet, the cycling ahead no longer seemed as unsavory as it had before. We had decided to take the shorter and flatter of the two routes through Cleveland and beyond. We had learned that this route also traversed the seedier neighborhoods, but it was faster. And it wasn't as if the area we were to travel through had a corner on crime in the city.

As we began traveling toward the city from the west, the Cleveland skyline on Lake Erie beckoned us on a beautiful day. A bike path ushered us onto a city street headed straight for downtown. Unlike the dead insect in our motel room, my antennae were alive and well. The butterflies within were evidence of this. We continued through a dense residential area without hesitation. We weren't about to dilly-dally. People on porches and steps watched with interest, some more than others. Some called out, but we just kept riding. And we had yet to reach the more troubled area.

Soon, we arrived in the heart of downtown, which was surprisingly tranquil at ten o'clock in the morning. There was little traffic—just tall buildings and concrete everywhere. I wondered how out of place we looked with our heavy loads and camping gear aboard. We would certainly be hard to miss with our bright yellow and red panniers, and high-visibility cycling regalia. I just hoped we wouldn't be a target, especially as we traveled through the more impoverished residential areas. We found comfort in the familiar surroundings of yesterday's excursion to the city. The straightforward route through town soon led to a bicycle path in an abandoned industrial area east of the city. We were lakefront, with splendid views of dark blue Lake Erie to our left. Miles of secluded bike path appeared ahead. An occasional fellow traveler rode toward us, reassuring us of an optimistic end to this trail.

Riding up the east side of the city landed us into one of Cleveland's most affluent areas. Gates surrounded immaculately manicured grounds and multimillion-dollar mansions where surely wealthy corporate executives or star athletes lived. Dense tree cover provided some natural landscaping while shielding the estates from the direct sun and camouflaging them from passersby. Strategically placed commercial landscaping complemented the high, ornate fences while masking other security systems. These security systems were apparently tasked with securing the insecure within. The well-guarded homes seemed extravagant and materialistic, but also distant and cold, imprisoned in their steel cages. *Who would live here?* I thought. *Perhaps someone who wants others to know they live here, but are frightened to death their exposed earthly treasure would vanish?* Shortly, we left the high-end for the low-end—with nothing in between but a gate.

The neighborhood to the east was impoverished and depressed—and it went on for miles. People milling about seemed downcast, heavy-hearted, or just plain angry. Buildings begging for facelifts lined the boulevard, as did well-traveled vehicles with dull, dinged-up finishes. The road had seen many miles since its last tune-up, with its age spots and wrinkles masquerading as potholes, cracks, and crevices. There hadn't been a new dollar invested here in years, or so it appeared. Those had been spent miles behind us, just the other side of the gate.

It seemed that people on both sides of the gate had to be stuck. Why else would they stay? But, then again, many were probably born into these conditions and had not discovered, or been able to attain, a better life. Perhaps some had strong family ties and responsibilities. Perhaps others lacked the resources, insights, or strength to break free. Still others might have lacked the courage and faith to escape, or even the belief or understanding that they could.

Their condition reminded me of my own dilemma months earlier. I was stuck in a different place, and it took great effort to break free. After all, inertia is a powerful but invisible force, and fear

Facing page: The Cleveland skyline

can be paralyzing. The easy answer was to do nothing—and die a slow, miserable death.

> This side of the gate reminded me of a mission trip to the inner streets of Philadelphia that I participated in years ago. I realized then that, as a follower of Jesus, I was called to be His hands and feet to the poor, the orphans, and the brokenhearted. Here we were, with our new bikes, whizzing by all three people groups, many of whom were on a death row of sorts. They might die a slow death such as Tim described above, or maybe a quick one from a random act of violence or suicide.
>
> When poverty confronts you, it demands a response other than simply passing through it, hoping to make it out alive, and forgetting about it thereafter. Our bike trip was affecting me at a deeper level than I could handle at times—and this was one of those times.

We were among the fortunate here. We had a way out, as long as they'd let us. And that's where we were headed while wasting no time to get there. We would escape the same way others would: by God's grace, His guiding hand, and our own resolve and strength. I just prayed there would be no mechanical failures, misinterpreted glances, or body language giving the natives opportunity or excuse to exploit our presence.

A favorite treatery

Our pace slowed and our spirits lightened as we pulled ourselves out of the depression. We met the shoreline of Lake Erie again and rode alongside it for miles. The weather was exquisite and the roads good. There was much to celebrate with this day's ride, and we did so with a special treat at yet another Dairy Queen. Thanks to flat terrain, a supportive tailwind off Lake Erie, a beautiful sun, and low humidity, we were on our way to a ninety-one-mile day. Our ride through the urban areas of Cleveland was complete and we would soon enter familiar terrain.

Late-afternoon ride along Lake Erie

On August 20, we left Ohio and the Midwest for good. Just as endless corn and soybean fields had dominated the Midwest, orchards along Lake Erie became commonplace, painting a different but nonetheless comparatively grand landscape. We bicycled along Lake Erie for days with none of its distant shores in sight. The northwest Pennsylvania panhandle hosted us for fifty miles, including an interesting tour through Erie, which boasts over 100,000 people. Before the day was out, we entered New York, which borders New England on its eastern flank. One more day along Lake Erie would position us for a ride into another large city, Buffalo.

Early the next day, a friendly cyclist joined Debbie for several miles while I was riding ahead of them. Seemed a family reunion was on the docket and she soon became an invited guest. With more miles to cover, she graciously declined. We rode on, chewing up more miles along the shore of Lake Erie, wondering when it would ever end.

We meandered past mansions with "for sale" signs on Lake Shore Drive. A late afternoon pit stop provided sufficient entertainment to carry us to our evening stop.

Bathrooms were elusive along the shore of Lake Erie. During a stop to fix a rattle on my bicycle, a woman on an ATV came by. Since my bladder was about to burst, I abruptly asked her if she knew where there was a bathroom.

"Sure," she said. "You can use the one in my house. I live just up there." She pointed a few houses up a side street.

Wasting no time, I followed her and found timely relief. She asked if she could refill my Camelbak with water, to which I agreed.

"Could you put ice in it, too?" I asked.

When our sincere helper returned, I noticed she had put the ice around the plastic pouch rather than in it. This brought smiles to our faces. Once out of sight, I quickly removed the ice to stop the trickle of ice-cold water down my back.

Toward the eastern end of Lake Erie, we could now catch a glimpse of the Buffalo skyline in the distance. We made our way to Hamburg, New York, and secured accommodations just before a downpour, narrowly averting rain yet again.

"International Flight"

Travel was beginning to feel mundane. As Debbie's back-to-school deadline approached, we had a decision to make. We were reminded of it when we stayed overnight on US Route 20 in New York. Several hundred miles to the east, just off Route 20, lay our home. We could abandon our bicycle maps and head straight east, or we could follow them into Canada and visit Niagara Falls. Canada, to the north, was in the wrong direction for a speedy trip home. And we would need to contend with border crossings, which could cost additional time. A direct route east might also avoid some mountain climbing. The direct route home would likely lop two to three days off our trip, but would not end at the Atlantic Ocean.

From a navigational standpoint, this was an easy decision: stick with the maps. We also expected the map routing would send us through beautiful territory. We were already familiar with the New England portion. But to follow the Adventure Cycling route would almost certainly make Debbie late for school. I had been to Niagara Falls in 2005 with my mother; Debbie hadn't been there since childhood. I knew she would love seeing the falls. And a border crossing on bicycles would certainly be unique. Heading to Niagara Falls could also change the character of our trip, which was in dire need of a boost.

We couldn't see getting this close to Niagara, an awesome natural phenomenon, only to abort the mission. And it certainly didn't seem reasonable to omit it from our extended honeymoon. If you are going to embark on a once-in-a-lifetime experience, you don't take short-cuts. Armed with this reasoning, we decided to stick with the maps.

One consequence of this decision was to pass through another major city. Our trip would be on a Sunday, if that were any consola-tion. How much trouble could one get into on a Sunday riding a bicycle through Buffalo? We were about to find out.

After church in Hamburg, we bicycled to Orchard Park for lunch, and then on toward Buffalo. We passed through some rundown neighborhoods and then another abandoned industrial area, just as we had through Cleveland. We encountered virtually no traffic in this area, but for an occasional car. Each beat-up car that traveled by made me uneasy. It was just us, them, and many vacant buildings. One block to our right, we saw run-down living quarters and some activity. Downtown lay just ahead in plain view. Nevertheless, we couldn't get there fast enough.

> Several blocks of our ride into Buffalo were downright eerie. This section was so abandoned it felt like we were completely alone—yet, there were many hiding places for wayward youth with too much time on their hands. Graffiti-etched, boarded-up buildings and empty sidewalks paved our pathway to downtown. Then a passing car or hollering from a block or two to the north reminded us of life—but also caused anxiety. It didn't feel like a very happy place.

Soon, we arrived in downtown Buffalo on the easternmost tip of Lake Erie. The Niagara River was about to take over from here, trans-porting millions of gallons of water downstream to please onlookers at Niagara Falls. But up first for us was the border crossing.

At the Buffalo border crossing, we were funneled with our loaded bikes through a large turnstile that resembled a revolving door with bars. At first, the turnstile seemed too tight for the cargo.

My bicycle tilted sideways and got caught. After some maneuvering, I was able to right the bike and guide it around the curve in the door. Once on the other side, I couldn't wait to capture Debbie's passage through the turnstile. But no sooner had I raised my camera, when a US customs official bounced out the door all in a dither. I had unwittingly breached a security measure in that area. When she threatened to confiscate my camera, I pleaded for mercy and quickly stowed it away. Meanwhile, Debbie had done a better job negotiating the turnstile with her bicycle.

Border-crossing regulations required that we walk our bikes across the long Peace Bridge that spanned the Niagara River, providing an excellent photo opportunity of intriguing views of the Buffalo skyline, Lake Erie, the Niagara River, and Fort Erie on the Canadian side. The Niagara River connects Lake Erie to Lake Ontario. While adjacent lanes of traffic hosting hundreds of cars in either direction sat with their motorists impatiently waiting for their turn at the border, we stood atop the Peace Bridge and guzzled in the panoramic views.

Buffalo from the Peace Bridge

Balancing a heavily loaded bicycle on a narrow sidewalk with one hand while taking pictures with the other felt precarious. Could I trust my one-handed grip and the thin camera strap as I raised the camera over and beyond the chest-high bridge railing? Hundreds of feet beneath us lay water collected from four of the Great Lakes, awaiting its turn to plunge violently over the tumultuous falls downstream. Several quick shots would be satisfactory, as this unique opportunity overruled any irrational feelings about losing the priceless portfolio of pictures captured on the digital card within. After all, our feet were firmly planted on concrete, despite the sway and rumble felt when tractor trailers resumed their march toward the border station.

After taking pictures, we continued our privileged pathway toward customs. Ours was a speedier journey, despite walking. A tunnel under the bridge on the Canadian side whisked us to a kiosk at the crossing, with only a few cars in line. When our turn came, the customs agent asked a few questions, but showed little interest in examining the contents of

The Peace Bridge spans the Niagara River

our panniers. Clearly, we were out of place, as hundreds of motorized vehicles remained queued in both directions. I wondered what the interrogation might look like to the frazzled motorists behind us. After a brief review of our credentials, our Canadian adventure began.

Attractive homes on well-groomed grounds lined the Canadian side of the Niagara River. As we rode along the Niagara Recreational Trail, the larger hotels at the falls soon appeared on the overcast horizon from miles upstream. The trail's close proximity to the river, and its boardwalks over some of the water, provided unique views of the falls and the surrounding area. The trip to the falls was easy—and not just because of the flat terrain. With the international flavor, the novelty of Niagara Falls, and its tourist attractions now in view, we were feeling renewed. The surroundings were breathing new life into us and our escapade.

The Niagara River sports two major falls: the American Falls and the more prominent Canadian, or Horseshoe, Falls.

Approaching Niagara Falls from upriver

The Niagara River at the base of the falls

Concrete structures built years ago to harness the power of water from four of the Great Lakes line the banks of the river. Downstream, the water flows through the narrow and deep Niagara River on its way to Lake Ontario, the St. Lawrence River, and the Atlantic Ocean.

At first, we saw, and then soon felt, the cool spray generated by the thunderous crashing of millions of gallons of water into the base of the falls. What appeared from afar like steam rising from boiling water became a misty shower to passersby. Tourists with cameras strapped around their necks had gathered, gawking at this astounding natural phenomenon. We joined in the amazement.

It soon occurred to us that not many of the thousands of people enjoying the falls had arrived by bicycle. We wheeled our heavy loads through the crowds along the mist-drenched walkways, with the cool spray continuing to fall like super-charged dew. We saw and heard people of all colors and tongues. Couples nestled one another closely, while excited youngsters darted ahead of their distracted parents, speaking more foreign

Canadian, or Horseshoe, Falls

words than this foreign land could understand. Tour buses deposited onlookers at the falls with the efficiency of a commuter line. Yet, once off the bus, people seemed relaxed. Smiles abounded. We had meandered into a grand menagerie of delightful coexistence where participants were captivated and entertained. Political agendas, racial tensions, domestic discord, and financial constraints had not made the trip—they were not welcome here.

The Niagara Falls tourism area on the Canadian side of the border was an interesting place, filled with people, attractions, and activity. It is a famous vacation area for tourists worldwide, notably for romantics. The fancier hotels would command a fascinating view of the falls, but would be much more expensive than the lower-end motels. As newlyweds, we were prime candidates to revel in the amenities, despite a timeframe of less than twenty-four hours.

As our trip approached its final leg, an overnight stay overlooking the falls seemed appropriate. Since we still had a gift card from our wedding for a five-star hotel, we decided to check the pricing and availability. Was Niagara Falls about to host the most luxurious stay of our entire trip?

Our loaded bicycles seemed just as out of place in the lobby of the splendid hotel as we did wearing our helmets and sweaty biking apparel. Workers in formal wear strutted about on the plush carpet looking for services to provide and the tips that would follow. Through the glass beyond, just outside, were the magnificent falls. There we were, wondering whether a few hours at a high-class hotel overlooking spectacular Niagara Falls was worth whatever it might cost, and even whether we would be welcomed with our greasy machines in tow. We were also doubtful our standard request for a first-floor room would be feasible. We gently rested our bicycles against the luxurious woodwork, scanning the room suspiciously for objections from the establishment. There were none, so I approached the front desk.

I placed the standard first-floor room request. *How can we possibly fit these bicycles in the elevator?* I thought. The trainee behind the counter stated they did not have any first-floor rooms. In fact,

Fireworks over Niagara Falls

they did not even have a first floor! The rooms started on the "sixth" floor and he had one available with a partial view of the falls. When I explained we could not easily transport our bicycles up to the "sixth" floor, he suggested the elevator. I remained skeptical that our loaded bicycles would fit, but pursued the possibility further. After we pleaded for the forty-six-dollar breakfast buffet to be included with the room charge, the desk manager eventually approved the discount. Her concession allowed us to purchase the room with our gift card plus the cash equivalent to what we had paid for many of the rooms on our trip. And, then, to my utter disbelief, the elevators were large enough to fit one loaded bike at a time.

We only had a few hours at Niagara Falls, but we made the most of it. We were even able to fit in a load of laundry while we watched the ten o'clock fireworks over the American Falls. A full moon presided. The ambiance was festive, but also romantic. A late-night dinner to live music on the patio of an Italian restaurant put tired bodies, and miles yet to travel, to rest. A transfixing kaleidoscope of colors shone forth from behind the illuminated falls, or so it appeared. A leisurely falls-side walk to the constant sound of rushing water preceded nestling into our bed in lovely accommodations overlooking the falls. Tonight was about us—a far cry from camping in the wild and some of the low-budget motels of weeks gone by. I loved it!

The next morning's breakfast buffet fueled our ride back across the border into New York state. First, however, we had more to see. On our way out of town, we rode through the Clifton Hill area, which offers the tourist an excessive dose of quick entertainment,

Clifton Hill

competing for their very last dollar in carnival-like fashion.

Plenty of accommodations, restaurants, and entertainment establishments supplement the natural beauty and allure of the falls. There are boats named *Maid of the Mist* that transport cellophane-wrapped tourists to the base of both falls, providing them with a Niagara shower courtesy of the drenching spray that rises from the tumultuous plunge of water over the falls. When the sun is shining, a rainbow often appears in the mist rising from the Canadian Falls.

Farther downstream from the falls appears a long gorge cut over the course of many years by this powerful flowage. At one sharp bend in the river, the Aero Car transports tourists on a cable suspended high across the river. As the Aero Car crawls across the gorge, power jet boats thrill tourists by slewing into

Aero Car and jet boats in Whirlpool

American Falls with its "Bridal Veil" on the right

the Niagara Whirlpool many feet below. Yet farther downstream near old power stations that still process electricity for the region, a botanical garden and a clock made from its flowers gave us one last taste of the Niagara experience.

The return border crossing on the Queenston-Lewiston Bridge came with a couple of twists. We had difficulty locating the bicycle access point to the border crossing. Following road signs, we rode several miles away from customs to a road that queued cars back toward the crossing. However, bicycles were prohibited! Confused by the apparent ambiguity, we backtracked. As we returned to the river and customs, we discovered a small,

Flower clock

inconspicuous entrance through a concrete barrier marked with an unobtrusive sign denoting the border entry point for bicyclists.

Once on the other side of the barriers, we spoke with a Canadian customs official who encouraged us to ride our bikes between the lengthy lines of traffic until we reached one of the border crossing booths. He said the motorists might be upset and yell or honk their horns at us, but to ignore them and go to the front. Bolstered by his authority, we unabashedly rode directly to the front through the narrow gap between two lanes of traffic, dodging mirrors and door handles along the way. Our fellow travelers expressed no overt ill will.

Our first attempt to insert ourselves into the front of the line was rejected, but a cycler-friendly motorist one lane over enthusiastically welcomed us to cut in front of him. The whole carload was impressed with our loads and our long trek from the West Coast. The customs agent's interrogation was as hassle-free as it had been in Buffalo. We were soon on our way.

With still many miles to travel before landing at the Atlantic, I was relieved that we were ushered to the front of the line at Lewiston. Judging from the number and length of the lanes of traffic, we would have been stuck at the border for hours. What a great feeling to catapult to the front of the line. But now, of course, we needed to cross New York state, second in mileage only to Montana on our long trip. And school started in a week!

I must have been short on sleep because, after crossing back into America, I took another wrong turn. Wrong turns are a part of touring and certainly forgivable, but this decision led us down a very steep grade. The ride down was wonderful, but when reality hit, the ride back up was brutal. To make matters worse, we were short on time, the weather was raw, and the skies were threatening. Debbie was most always forgiving, but I knew she wasn't happy about having to climb back up that hill. For that matter, neither was I!

Tim did a great job navigating, but he did lead us astray a few times. In Portland, Oregon, my intuition was to travel straight through the intersection. Tim read the map literally and turned right. Several miles later, after we had become lost in an industrial park, he realized the mistake and reversed direction. I let that one go.

Leaving Indiana, we took a delightful side trip toward Fort Wayne when the sun, acting as compass, raised concerns. I had no idea we were off course, so I was grateful when he realized the error and turned around.

But the two faux pas on the same day when leaving Niagara Falls took the cake. Although I didn't say anything at the time, I would rather have avoided the extra mileage and climbing.

We continued to avoid rain in most unusual ways. We were expecting a soaking. The skies for the past two days were cloudy and our blog followers had made comments of stormy weather ahead. My navigational gaffes caused a delay that helped us miss another downpour as we made our way to the Erie Canal system.

The following day, we rode alongside the canal. The state of New York keeps the archaic canal operating during tourist season. A path accompanies the canal where bicyclists can ride on a predominantly crushed gravel surface for many miles, avoiding traffic and hills. Portions of the Erie Canal provide a tranquil setting for riding, while other portions are less aesthetic and less bicyclist-friendly.

It was hard to believe this docile, narrow body of water was at one time the lifeblood of the Industrial Revolution in America, transporting goods back and forth to the Great Lakes. It seemed so small by today's standards. We spotted old barges, tugs, and other equipment from yesteryear dotted along the route. Fresh paint jobs, restored locks, and manicured banks gave an unconvincing impression that commerce had once moved through these waters, despite the fact it did. Although perhaps an engineering marvel of its time, we were riding beside a dinosaur—but an interesting and ironically pastoral relic nonetheless.

Facing page: Cycling along the Erie Canal

Higher ground

Lake Ontario

We eventually made our way east of Rochester to Pittsford, where I lived during junior and senior high school. A quick detour to the family home added more nostalgia. Seeing the old homestead ever so briefly, however, brought back mixed emotions. It was here, at fifteen years of age, that I began a long downhill spiral into eating disorders, namely anorexia and then bulimia. And the seeds of my alcoholism were planted back then. I wonder what might have happened had I made different choices. The right choices, of course, would have been obvious had I known God. Even then, He was trying to reach me, at the Servant's Quarters, a Christian coffeehouse downtown. I knew God was real, and I made overtures toward a commitment to Him then, but nothing stuck. I was too distracted. I would need to experience more pain before I would recognize and respond to His love for me. I struggled for fourteen years before I got on my knees and asked God to take away the eating disorders. Six months later, I stopped purging and have been free ever since.

Of all the places a random cross-country journey could have taken me, it seemed rather amazing—in fact, too amazing, too coincidental—that I found myself back here, even on my honeymoon, as a reminder of where I had come from, and more importantly, what God had delivered me from. But it was, and is, a new day. And there is no more need to look back, to be encumbered by past demons. For, to do so makes steering on the path ahead more difficult. Rather, I have a bright future—an awesome future, I am sure—even though I don't yet know what it offers. All I know is God delivered me from my past, and has given me peace and the assurance of His care. And my riding partner, though he may not always realize it, is a constant reminder of God's deliverance in my life. Yes, the old is gone. And I will never be the same. Praise be to God!

The next day, we headed away from the canal, north toward Lake Ontario, the easternmost of the Great Lakes. Like Lake Erie, the Lake Ontario region is a land of orchards. Whereas grapes were the primary fruit in the Lake Erie region, apples were now the main crop, with a smattering of peaches and pears. The terrain had also changed and civilization was thinning out. Despite some hills getting in our way, we eked out seventy-eight miles, eclipsing 3,000 for the entire trip—not bad for a couple of old-timers!

Debbie had improved her pace since the start of our trip much more than I had. As our remaining mileage was winding down, she was winding up.

Cruising through orchards

We were now capable of cranking out significant daily mileage, even in hilly terrain. We could sense the end approaching, conjuring up bittersweet feelings of saying good-bye to this glorious experience and hello to whatever lay ahead.

> I was looking forward to going home and back to school. I had so many experiences to share with family and friends. It was time to plug back into life as I had known it. But another part of me just wanted this to go on forever. I felt so free and alive—and incredibly close to the Lord, even as Tim and I grew closer each day.
>
> Later, I came to realize that life as I had known it was gone forever. Not only had Tim undergone great change, but, in order for us to build a new life together, I would need to change too. We tend to become set in our ways as we get older. Although change may be more difficult, that doesn't mean it can't or shouldn't happen. When we stop changing, we stop growing.
>
> Adjusting to married life has helped me grow. God works powerfully through holy matrimony. It hasn't always been easy, but it has always been good. I have grown personally and spiritually. Tim has too. Although we both enjoyed our single days and benefited from them, we agree that being married has enriched our lives.

From my perspective, I didn't want this adventure to end. I had been stuck behind a desk for too many years. I was recapturing the joy of my youth. Although the bicycling had become very repetitious, seeing new places every day was stimulating enough not to stop. My muscles and aerobic capacity felt great, too. Having Debbie with me at every turn was so unique and satisfying. Returning to daily life would be a letdown. Nevertheless, I would have the opportunity to shape that daily life once this fantastic voyage ended.

Professionally, Debbie would return to a pre-defined existence. Mine, however, was a blank canvas. I would need to apply to my post-trip endeavors the same element of faith that had allowed us to thrive on this bicycle adventure. Faith provides comfort in the face of uncertainty, and peace and confidence amid challenges. Our bicycle adventure had been full of both. For Debbie and me, faith means to trust God with the uncertainties of our lives and to believe He will work all matters out for our spiritual betterment despite what troubles may befall us. I need this in my life always.

10. The Homestretch

LAKE ONTARIO, WITH ITS BILLOWY and threatening rain clouds, would soon escort us into the Adirondack region of upstate New York. The Adirondack region is a mountainous and heavily forested area, part of the Appalachian Mountain chain. We were about to return to some stiff climbs after weeks of predominantly flat riding. We were now in great shape. We were ready for this—in fact, we were on a mission to burn up the remaining mileage. But it would not come without a fight—a fight against our bodies, our machines, and our minds.

Cranking through the Adirondacks

The clouds on this particular day were downright intimidating. Goose bumps attested to the raw weather, sending us back to our panniers for warmer clothes. Nevertheless, we were programmed for miles. We had much ground to cover in only a few days. Thirty miles into the ride, we encountered just our second flat tire of the entire trip. It was my rear tire. We repaired the flat by replacing its tube. But no sooner had we ventured down the road than it went flat again. We had been too hasty to replace the tube without checking for the cause of the flat. When we removed the rear tire a second time, we discovered a tiny wire stuck in the tire. Another spare tube later, the air held. I might add that the second replacement occurred much faster than the first with Debbie operating the pump. It pays to marry a strong woman.

Not all was well, however. The new ride was lumpy, like a wad of bubblegum was stuck inside the tire. Deflating the tire and re-inflating it addressed the problem. We resumed our ride after a significant midday delay.

Our mechanical problem came with a side benefit. The dark clouds toward the east had passed. We rode ahead on damp

165

Ominous beauty

pavement through a desolate, forested area, but with no precipitation. We later discovered we had once again averted a downpour.

Our new surroundings came with few services. Areas like this made me appreciate our maps. It was difficult to envision much around the next corner, other than wildlife, trees, or streams. Knowing we were following a map reassured me we would arrive back in civilization before too long. We phoned ahead for accommodations and signed on for a stay at a furnished apartment. The deal was sealed when the proprietor offered us, sight unseen, use of the family car to travel to a restaurant for supper, as there were no eateries within walking distance. This was snowmobile country, and it was offseason. It reminded me of the more desolate areas in northern Maine—heavily wooded and nary a vehicle for miles.

When we arrived at the apartment, we were not disappointed in the facility, only our low mileage. At this juncture, a forty-seven-mile day felt like we had unfinished business. It had been one of those cool days where making headway seemed difficult. We would push harder on the accelerator tomorrow. The furnishings in our overnight nest were lovely. We even had a washer and dryer to tidy up our laundry.

An early start the next morning landed us at the Osceola Outpost for breakfast. We had a big day ahead, with plenty of hills and, hopefully, plenty of miles. We tanked up with a big breakfast and continued through the remote region. The sky was beautiful. Gone were the large ominous clouds of Lake Ontario. Blue sky shone overhead as we rolled through sunlit forests and crossed bridges over sparkling rivers and streams.

For the past few days, I had been hearing things. There was a distinct sound, like rubbing or chafing, coming from my running gear. It made me nervous. The bicycle shop in Missoula had verbally reprimanded me about the unusually heavy load I was expecting my bicycle to carry. Was there some truth to what they were saying, and the frame was weakening and beginning to flex too much? Or was the crank failing? Or was it simply the brakes rubbing? Maybe it was just my mind playing tricks on me. We had traveled over 3,000 miles and had as little as 500 left. How sad would it be to have a bicycle fail us now? Services seemed far away. I would examine the bicycle when the noise bothered me enough, but I was unable to identify the source of the sound. Interesting how hard it is to diagnose a problem when you are no longer on top of the bicycle pedaling it. I just said a prayer and resumed pedaling.

When we arrived in Boonville, Debbie went into a convenience store. Normally, I would join her, but I had already crossed the intersection. So, I randomly parked my bicycle across the street against a convenient prop, an office building. As I was standing there thinking, a man came out of the building to talk. He was an avid bicyclist and took an interest in our trip. I explained my concern about the sound I was hearing. Just then, another fellow, an acquaintance of the first, came walking by. This individual had just rebuilt a bicycle, which gave him immediate credibility as a bicycle mechanic. He looked at the bicycle, tested the crank, and concluded the bottom bracket inside the crank was wearing out. He thought there would be no issue, however, in continuing to ride it for the remainder of the trip. In his estimation, the bicycle would get me home with no problems.

We continued our ride with his reassurance. Next up was Old Forge, a resort town and destination for travelers riding up Route 28 to escape the metropolitan New York area. We would join the tourists for a time and earn a reprieve from the backwoods feel of the past fifty miles. After a delightful lunch in town, we headed out for Inlet and the eastern side of Fulton Chain Lakes.

Minutes from the restaurant, and still within town limits, we noticed a fawn grazing on a lawn. The fascination of wildlife in a relatively busy town attracted other onlookers, too. The fawn acted nonchalant, apparently accustomed to the many tourists who frequent the area. After spending several minutes enjoying our Bambi sighting, we ventured down a lakeside road where we spotted other deer unconcerned about their surroundings. At one such spot in the road, Debbie came face to face, within twenty feet, of a doe. Not even a passing car could separate them as they stared spellbound at one another.

We arrived at Inlet, a resort pit stop with a bicycle shop. The continuous rubbing and chafing sound had been getting worse. It was again weighing on my mind. So, I decided to get another opinion on the bicycle. Surely, this Trek dealer would be able to advise me. The owner of the shop just happened to be stopping by. He looked at my bike, examined the brakes, and decided to take it for a test ride. He concluded that a rear brake pad was rubbing. Meanwhile, since cell service was lacking and daylight waning, the staff at the shop called ahead to reserve a room for us at a motel just up the road. In their words: "You'll love it. It's a real dive, but you'll love it!" We weren't quite sure what that meant, but we were mostly interested in a bed and a roof over our heads. It had both. After a minor adjustment to the brake pad, we resumed our ride.

Less than a mile up the road, the sound returned, or perhaps just resumed. Maybe the analysis by the stranger in Boonville was more accurate. If it was the bottom bracket, we weren't going to replace it now. And since the brakes worked fine, this was a problem for

Dear meets deer, Old Forge, New York

another day. My mind had been working overtime on this issue, and more pressing matters were at hand. Sunset was upon us with several more miles to reach our destination.

When we arrived after sundown, we immediately checked in at the bar. Noise was at a fever pitch, as patrons reveled with their like-minded conversationalists. The strong smell of alcohol permeated the close quarters. As I approached the bar, the bartender threw down a shot of liquor. I knew he didn't want anyone to see him, but I had. Someone more comfortable with this environment might have exposed him with eyes wide open or a smart remark, but I chose not to. All we needed was a room for the night and no trouble. *What have we gotten ourselves into?* I thought. I paid him forty dollars for the room and then we lifted our bikes, loaded and all, up a long set of creaking stairs.

At the head of the stairs was a semicircular common area, trimmed with antiquated woodwork and used primarily for storage. Surrounding the common area were rooms for rent. A small hallway to the right led to our corner room. We pushed open the door and found vintage 1940s furniture and plumbing. At the head of the bed was curved wrought iron supported by vertical iron slats. A

Time warp!

similar but smaller structure was located at the foot of the bed. The mattress, of comparable vintage, had a squishiness that gave its unsuspecting prey the feeling of being slowly swallowed up in quicksand. In the opposite corner of the small room, a portable desk fan, woefully undersized for the task at hand, rested on top of a large, upright, steam radiator. Nestled in the corner was an old dresser crowned with a large mirror, such as one might find in great grandma's bedroom. I gave the awkward and archaic push-out iron windows a try to coax some air into the stuffy room.

On the inside wall was the entrance to a bathroom shared by an adjoining room. The old-fashioned, freestanding bathtub within had a makeshift shower nozzle annexed to the plumbing, with a wraparound curtain intended to contain the water inside the tub. Management had posted a small but conspicuous note on the mirror to help prevent embarrassing encounters with the stranger next door. As I tried to decipher the confusing instructions and contemplated the establishment's plan to limit access to this shared bathroom, I thought, *I sure hope they don't have an inebriated guest next door.* Based on what I had seen and heard downstairs, this seemed like a probable outcome. Surely, someone would be locked out of the bathroom tonight. I was hopeful it would not be me or, worse yet, my wife.

Meanwhile, we could still hear the clamor from the bar downstairs. Debbie decided to stay in the room while I went outside to fire up the stove to heat some freeze-dried beef stroganoff. I found myself in the midst of drunken folks who were making bad conversation, the type of discussion that goes on for hours with seemingly no end in sight and no reason for being, and stilted with a touch of one-upmanship.

I finished my chores and went back upstairs. The bartender had told us to leave our bicycles in the common area, but we had taken them into the room anyway. We were confident we would not damage the property. Besides, it was easier to manage our belongings with the bikes inside the room. And we didn't need to worry about what could happen to them outside, especially in this setting.

Bedtime was fast approaching. We wondered what kind of sleep we might manage in this bed and in this ruckus. Any movement on the jelly-like mattress created a wave that was sure to disturb any bedfellow. As if the wave were not bad enough, an accompanying squeak in the springs below was sure to disturb anyone who rented the adjacent room, unless of course they were drop-dead drunk. In an effort to get adequate rest and prevent one another from rolling off the bed, we settled in like cadavers, minimizing any movement until we were both asleep. After a long day of biking, falling asleep was easy even under these circumstances.

The following morning, the chaos and clamor in the bar was gone. Daylight shone brightly within. The breakfast cook asked if we had brought our bikes into our room. She was concerned because they had just installed new carpets. If the carpet was new, it certainly played a subdued role in the room's décor. Nevertheless, I calmly assured her we left no trace. After partaking in the breakfast special, which included some complimentary homemade cornbread, it was time to vamoose.

We left our one-of-a-kind experience behind, returning to a pristine adventure more befitting of the natural beauty of the region. Somehow, the prior evening had felt like an initiation into a club, a dreaded but required ritual for passage to the other side. Nevertheless, the throwback in time added to the adventure. Perhaps it was an

We awoke to a beautiful day in a scenic region

obligatory christening into the ranks of adventure cyclists.

The Adirondack region's many lakes provided a striking contrast of colors against their green mountain drapery on a bright sunny day. The landscape was wonderful to behold. We proceeded to Blue Mountain Lake and one of the more challenging climbs of the entire trip. We wiggled our bicycles up the long grade as tourist traffic whizzed by. This would be a day of climbs and descents. One stretch of road was magnificently surrounded by trees and mountains—nothing but. We traveled for miles and hours without seeing any manmade structures. Except for an infrequent vehicle, it was just our luscious surroundings and us. Later in the day, another deer in the road surprised Debbie.

After a long day climbing through the mountains, there is nothing quite like a long downhill ride, feeling the breeze against your face and that sense of freefall in the heart. Gravity has its advantages. We had no idea, however, just how hair-raising this passion could become until we landed atop a hill outside of Ticonderoga, New York, at dusk after eighty-plus miles. We had pulled off the road to dig out our lights before descending the hill. I asked Debbie to get the lights out of her pannier, and she insisted I had them.

While we rummaged through stuff sacks and debated who put the lights away last, a vehicle pulled up and told us it was all downhill into Ticonderoga, albeit for a few miles. They offered to trail us and illuminate our path with their vehicle's headlights. Their escort would help shield us from other motorists who may have been unable to see us in the dark. So, rather than sending these Good Samaritans away and continuing a frustrating and, as yet, unproductive search in the dark for lights, we readily accepted their offer. Besides, both their headlights and their taillights would protect us better than our lights could. For the record, I later discovered that I had the lights.

So, off we went, like skydivers out of a plane. Debbie soon found her love of the freefall pushing her faster than anticipated down the hill, well beyond our newfound friends' headlights. I was busy pulling and squeezing brake levers, trying to slow my runaway bike.

West of Ticonderoga, a peaceful sunset belies the wild ride ahead

Debbie was unable to slow her bike enough to re-emerge into the beams of our helpers' headlights. In fact, it was so dark and I was so concerned about keeping my own bike under control that I could no longer see her. I wondered, *Would a deer dart out of the darkness? Would either of us strike an unforeseeable obstacle or flaw in the pavement? Or would heat from the constant braking burn through a rim and blow a tire?* What I didn't think of at the time, thank goodness, was the unthinkable: whether there might be a curve in the road.

With the combination of a heavy load, a steep hill, and utter blindness, we were riding on the edge, on the verge of an impending disaster! After several minutes, my hand strength had virtually disappeared. It had been a long day and the chronic tingling and numbness we had developed in our hands over the course of the trip had taken its toll. Even as that out-of-control feeling was settling in, yellow diamond-shaped truck grade signs flew by—first one, then another, and another, until I lost count. The yellow flashes flew by so fast that we were unable to see the grade percentage on each one. Perhaps this was just as well.

Finally, and mercifully, we reached the bottom and the panicky feeling subsided. We were back in control. And we had survived. Having completed their mission, we thanked our Good Samaritans and watched them vanish into the night, nameless but not forgotten. They left as mysteriously as they had come—just at the appointed time.

We were thankful for safe passage down the monster hill outside of Ticonderoga. This descent dropped 900 feet in three miles, finalizing the 6,000 feet of declining altitude enjoyed on this roller-coaster day. Even with all of the braking, we had been freefalling at twenty miles per hour down the hill.

> Wow! What a rush! I couldn't believe the steepness of the grade. Almost immediately, the bike took off—I couldn't stop it. My hands were killing me. So, I just enjoyed the ride. It was a long hill—I wasn't sure it was ever going to end. When we reached the bottom, I was relieved—but I also enjoyed the thrill. I'll never forget that ride. I just wish I could have seen it!

By day's end, my cycling computer registered over 3,800 feet climbed and 4,700 calories burned. Eighty-six miles in terrain like this spoke well for our conditioning. Despite the accomplishments of the day, including crossing the Hudson River and landing on the New England border, our downhill ride just after dusk was the most memorable event of all, forever seared into our memories.

Our dark ride down the hill outside of Ticonderoga teaches a lesson. There are times when you may have difficulty seeing your way through life. There are times when you simply don't know what is ahead of you—in fact, more times than we like to think. There are also times when our circumstances wrest the last vestiges of control from us. But that does not mean you stop—and once you get going, sometimes you can't stop, no matter how hard you try. What it does suggest is that people will come alongside to help and encourage you. And at some point, you must let go of your worries and trust that the path ahead has been prepared for you—and you for it. Sometimes, you just need to exercise faith. And, of course, the object in which you invest your trust will either warrant it or fail you miserably.

At least for Debbie and me, we choose to trust God with our uncertainties and fears.

New England Soil

How did Tim get out here so fast? I thought. Then I realized it wasn't Tim and those weren't our bikes, although they could have passed for our panniers. A cyclist was pumping up his wife's tires on the morning after descending into Ticonderoga. We exchanged pleasantries and lauded the benefits of the Ortlieb panniers. When his wife approached, she said, "I've spoken with three or four people who have been on multiple tours and are talking about doing more. I can't wait to get this over with."

I agreed with her about finishing the current tour. For one thing, I couldn't wait to share this with my family and friends. We hadn't had much time for that along the way. I missed them. Part of being reunited would be describing what life had been like for the past two months. There was so much to celebrate and I wanted to share it with them. But, deep inside, I thought, *Hmmmm—people do this more than once?*

By light of day, we could see Ticonderoga, a small, picturesque town nestled between the Adirondack Mountains and Lake Champlain. We knew we were getting closer to home when we discovered the pastor at the Cornerstone Alliance Church hailed from Maine. After post-service discussions about TheHopeLine with him and his wife, we headed out for what we thought would be a leisure day. We had ridden 165 miles in the last two days through hilly terrain and needed to take it easy before more climbing to come in Vermont and New Hampshire.

First up was nearby Fort Ticonderoga, which played a prominent role in the American Revolution. It was here Ethan Allen had led the Green Mountain Boys to victory over the British. We enjoyed lovely views of Lake Champlain and Lake George to the south, but were itching for the ferry ride across Lake Champlain. This trip had it all!

Fort Ti Ferry

The ferry, as it turned out, was nothing more than a barge guided along a cable. It fit up to eighteen cars and shuttled back and forth between New York and Vermont all day long during the summer. It even came with its own apple stand. A two-dollar fare for this border crossing seemed more than reasonable. After pleasantly sliding across a narrow portion of the lake, we rolled onto the New England soil of the Green Mountain State.

We weren't home yet, but it sure was beginning to look and feel that way. As the crow flies, we were within about 200 miles of home. If we had a problem now, we still couldn't walk home. But odds were good someone we knew could help us. We were also entering the geographic footprint of the company from which I had just retired. We had friends here who would help us. This was familiar territory.

But our bicycle gear was still haunting me. The rubbing and chafing sound continued from my bike. Debbie's bicycle hadn't had a brake job yet. And although my brakes had been replaced in Great Falls, Montana, I rode them regularly down descents, including the previous night's scary ride. I knew from the terrain, let alone the map, we had some steep grades in front of us. The topographic map looked like a virtuoso pianist's four long, slender fingers. Two of these grades, straight up and straight down, were in Vermont. Two others, not quite as steep, were in New Hampshire. Bicyclists have died when losing control on steep descents, so I didn't think it wise to find ourselves at the top of these climbs without adequate brakes to slow downhill speed.

The last of these climbs would be the longest and highest, the Kancamagus Highway. I have climbed the Kancamagus before, but never from the steeper west side and certainly not with a load like the one I was carrying. We were so close now. I don't know if it was stage fright or a crisis of confidence, but getting this close and not finishing haunted me.

We also needed to refine our endpoint and timetable. People who were following us were interested. We weren't sure whether this would draw them to meet us or whether their curiosity was just getting the better of them. Regardless, we were most concerned about getting Debbie back to work. It was Sunday, August 30, and school started with a half day on Tuesday. We wouldn't be back by then even if we bolted for home immediately. With some lovely landscape ahead, however, we weren't about to consider aborting the mission in favor of riding through the crazy traffic of Massachusetts.

Our leisure day of riding was anything but. Much of the difficulty stemmed from narrow roads with rough pavement. Summer traffic on a beautiful Vermont day was challenging coming into Middlebury, a small college town readying for another school year. Nevertheless, our ride through the western portion of the state featured long, gorgeous vistas back across the Champlain Valley toward New York in the west, where the Adirondack Mountains treated us to an encore performance. By late afternoon, we had lugged our tired bodies into Middlebury.

My continued paranoia about our equipment caused us to stop at a local bicycle shop. The owner was just closing for the day, but agreed to take a quick look at our brakes. He described the road ahead. The climb up Middlebury Gap had been under construction. It was a difficult climb and, if construction hadn't been completed, would be even more so. We frankly wondered what we would find. We also wondered whether we should tackle it immediately or get a better rest and add it to the following day's agenda.

The bike shop owner assured us our brakes were ample to handle what hills were left in our trip. We headed toward the gap and located a restaurant on the outskirts of town. After eating, and despite logging our lowest daily mileage of the entire trip, we decided to stay overnight on this side of the climb. Seven weeks ago in Idaho, we came to a different conclusion on another lazy Sunday. Perhaps we had grown wiser, but it was also apparent Debbie was exhausted. Accommodations were right here, right now, or an unknown number of miles over the climb. With daylight surely to wane, it was time to regroup and plan our final stages.

Once at the motel, and totally spent, Debbie crashed for the evening. I sat on the porch outside, looking into the night wondering what the final days would be like. It was time to lock down an itinerary. I wondered how many miles we could cover each day in the mountainous terrain of Vermont and New Hampshire. And I thought about where on the Atlantic coastline we should end. If we followed the cycling maps, we would need several more days before arriving at Bar Harbor and Acadia National Park. That would be awesome—to end this trip where our larger adventure had begun, where I had proposed to Debbie.

However, a triumphant end riding to the top of Cadillac Mountain wasn't going to happen. Debbie was adamant about returning to school as soon as possible. Although it is pleasing to be married to someone with a high sense of responsibility who takes her job seriously, it seemed ironic with Debbie's love for spontaneity and adventure that she was steering this ship back to the port of commonplace in the harbor of everyday life. It was nonsense to dwell on this now. I had logistics to address. We had received not one, but two, generous offers to help us home—offers we couldn't refuse. I needed to select one and make the necessary arrangements.

With the timing and vicinity of the end of our trip now resolved in my mind, I e-mailed our followers with the news. We would arrive in the Portland, Maine, area most likely in the late afternoon or evening of Wednesday, September 1. I would connect with some friends tomorrow to firm up the details. As Debbie lay sound asleep inside, I now believed she would arrive at school in just over three days. I felt lonely and sad on the porch. The end of our fantastic voyage was undeniably in sight, as much as I hated to admit it.

Final Climbs

The weather on the next morning was exquisite. A good night's sleep suggested we were ready to take on the first of the day's two steep climbs. The Appalachian Mountain chain continues in Vermont with the Green Mountains. With hills true to their name this time of year, we had struck the scenery jackpot when all shades of rich green hues popped into view. The visual sensation was like the green rush one experiences when first walking into Fenway Park. As we headed east through narrow roads intermittently shrouded in forest canopies, we delighted in magnificent views of the mountains, the sound of trickling waters splashing on rocks, the fresh scents in the air, and the small towns that define Vermont. When the

Tim cruises through the Green Mountain State

Vermont's challenging grades

canopies yielded to the bright sunshine, greener-than-green hills and smaller-than-small farming operations added to the quaint Vermont ambiance.

We tackled Middlebury Gap in Green Mountain National Forest early in the day and later flew down its eastern side, dropping 1,200 feet in just three miles. The second climb was so steep we considered dismounting our bikes. We were in great riding shape and carrying less weight than out West, but the painfully steep grade slowed us to a crawl while we tended to traffic in both directions. Although the hills were short compared to a climb like Lolo Pass, they were clearly steeper and more difficult. Once over the top, cracked pavement and curvy roads made for treacherous, plunging grades and titillating descents. As if the freefall weren't enough, worn brake shoes added a psychological twist. Some of the grades we encountered were in the 13 to 14 percent range.

As we ambled up one steep grade, a small rattletrap-like pickup truck came alongside. The driver offered us a place to overnight just over the hill. You might say he caught us off guard. We weren't exactly in a situation conducive to great conversation because we needed to dedicate every ounce of oxygen to power us up the hill. Our schedule also required we ride many more miles before stopping for the night. And we weren't totally sold on the authenticity of his offer. He seemed too intent in hearing a response. As we gasped for air, he failed to realize we had more pressing matters at hand.

Debbie contemplates the steep descent ahead

After I provided a breath-shortened "no thanks," he squealed his tires and shot up the remainder of the hill, leaving us behind to taste, if not choke on, his blue cloud of smoke. We had apparently spoiled his evening. Somewhere near the coast of Oregon, his long-lost cousin sat plotting his next prey's demise.

> By the time we reached Vermont, we had the bathroom breaks down to a science, or so we thought. On this day, I met the granddaddy of awkward moments.
> On an urgent nature call, we pulled onto a dirt road that appeared to offer adequate seclusion.
> Tim soon announced, "A car's coming." And almost immediately thereafter, "It's slowing down!"
> Nature, however, could not be denied. I dropped my pants and began taking care of business! The car pulled onto the dirt road. I sheepishly looked at the driver through his open window just a few feet away and said, "I'm sorry." Thankfully, the driver politely avoided eye contact and proceeded up what was apparently his driveway!

I owe Debbie a debt of gratitude for her flexibility and willingness to deal with "open air" restroom breaks. Rather than focusing on any embarrassment or awkwardness, she realized that it was part of the cost of enjoying our amazing trip across the country.

We ended the day on the border of New Hampshire thanks to a favorable tailwind. We had tallied seventy-five miles and climbed nearly 5,000 feet, our highest daily elevation gain of the entire trip. Yet, we had maintained a respectable speed of eleven miles per hour while enjoying the eye-popping scenery of one of the least populous states in our nation. Because we are New Englanders and familiar with these areas, it was easy to take their beauty for granted. However, the scenery on this day was impressive. If we could make it through New Hampshire tomorrow, we would be home free. Two more climbs would greet us in the morning. Another good night's sleep would do us well.

The Connecticut River separating New Hampshire and Vermont

After nearly two months of this routine, we had finally managed to slay late-morning starts in the interest of finishing well. Even as August drew to a close in New England, an early morning haze over the tranquil Connecticut River, which separates New Hampshire from Vermont, forewarned of a sultry day ahead. Crossing the Connecticut brought us into even more familiar territory—it felt like we were in our backyard ready for a victory lap. But that was premature. We rode north alongside the river until we reached the east-west route that would deliver us to Lincoln, a logical midpoint and lunch stop.

Climbing to splendid views in New Hampshire

New Hampshire's grades, although not quite as severe

as Vermont's, were longer and aesthetically more pleasing. After thirty-four miles, we had climbed to an altitude of 1,900 feet. At the top of our first climb, Debbie couldn't contain herself. She sped down the other side, leaving me behind. Miles later, I caught her at the bottom. We would drop 1,100 feet in six miles to arrive at Lincoln.

After lunch, we would need to climb another 2,100 feet over thirteen miles on the switchback-laden Kancamagus Highway, the last major climb of our trip. With dark clouds developing overhead, we wondered just how electrifying the remainder of the day would be. But we weren't stopping—it was time to stock up with plenty of fluids, as the mercury had pushed into the 90s. And it was muggy.

We stopped at a bagel shop for lunch. The generous shop owner gave us some bagels for the road. I muttered to Debbie, "We shouldn't take these; they will just add more weight and bulk." Herein lay the psychology of a bicyclist, wanting every edge as a daunting climb up a steep grade on an oppressively hot day awaited. Debbie easily convinced me to take the bagels. We filled our bottles and began our ascent toward Kancamagus Pass.

Debbie asked me not to announce the elevation levels as I had back at Lolo Pass. I rode behind her on the way up. We kept a steady pace and then slowed when we encountered the switchbacks. I was spinning in my lowest gear most of the way. Meanwhile, Debbie was very quiet yet obviously determined. She was in a zone. As we neared the top, I suddenly heard her exclaim, "Oh darn!"

I asked, "What's wrong?"

"I had to shift into my lower gear," she said.

Debbie tackles the Kancamagus

Upon further inquiry, I discovered she was talking about her more strenuous front gears, not the rear ones. While I had been crawling up the mountain trying to stay clear of traffic, she'd had plenty of lower gears in reserve. She was relying upon her strength and power as a personal challenge.

Debbie likes a challenge, for which I admire her. Naturally, I tried to blame my comparatively scant effort on the extra weight I was carrying, but that did not prove very persuasive. Moments later, we reached the top and celebrated by splitting one of those heavy bagels.

> I never experienced life so fully. Every day, together, we rode, worked, prayed, laughed, worshipped God, ate and drank, and slept. And, sometimes, we fought! But our togetherness brought us closer in the past two months than most people experience in years. While pedaling behind my new lifelong companion, Tim, the changing landscapes, the beauty of the sunsets, my incessant prayers, and God's protection deepened my faith, strengthened my body, enriched my life, and contented my soul—well, most of the time!

The climb up and down Kancamagus was undoubtedly the highlight of the most rewarding day of bicycling I have ever had. I couldn't have imagined the ease with which we dispatched of these hills when struggling up lesser hills on the first two days in Oregon, or treating saddle sores on our extended stay in Great Falls in mid-July. We would enjoy our victory lap tomorrow on a flat ride to the coast through southern Maine. The intimidating western flank of the mighty Kancamagus had whimpered harmlessly by the end of the day, with the long descent on the east side a just reward.

Traveling seventy-seven miles while climbing another 4,800 feet on a hot, humid day was an equally satisfactory prize—especially when we felt we had more miles in us when we stopped. We would save those for tomorrow. We had come a long way, but the end was nigh. The glee of conquering the last major climb on our trip would yield to a much different emotion as we nestled into bed at the White Deer Motel.

Melancholy had stepped into the room. This would be our last night on the road. No more honeymoon adventure, no more cycling, no more encounters with new and interesting places and people, and no more jaw-dropping landscapes. I didn't let on to Debbie, but I could have cried if I had let myself. In fact, I needed to fight back the tears, as my heart grew heavier. This adventure was ending. The emotional surge testified to that fact and to the grandeur of what we had experienced together. It felt a little bit like grief, which seemed inappropriate given the new life that lay ahead. Regardless, we would carry this with us forever—no one or no thing could ever take away what God had allowed us to share with one another.

> Just two days ago outside the Super 8 in Ticonderoga, I couldn't wait to be finished. But as we lay in bed on the final night, it was a much different story. I was overwhelmed with sadness. My feelings were so much stronger and deeper than my prior sentiment—which told me I would never get over this. *The joy is in the journey* kept running through my mind—and through the utter depth of my being. What we had shared together was nothing short of astounding. It made me realize the depth of God's love for me. I had all I could do to hold things together. But with Tim holding me tightly, I didn't want to dampen this larger-than-life moment with tears. Even though this journey was coming to an end, the marriage journey was just beginning!

Victory Lap

The final day of our trip went like clockwork. We were so fit that the unusually hot and humid 90-degree weather had little effect. We just needed fuel to keep the parts churning. We enjoyed a ride on fresh pavement through forests interrupted by intermittent farmland and water. The views were again lovely, albeit with the somewhat famil-iar look of home turf. The rustling sound of wild turkeys scurrying into the woods and fluttering to nearby branches rivaled the clicking of our gears and ticking of our wheels.

We had few concerns on this day. Not even bicycle maintenance issues would command the same power they had in past days. Despite a rear wheel out of true, the constant and mysterious rubbing sound, and well-worn brakes on both bikes, we knew these machines would not let us down.

As we approached the suburbs of Portland, heavy vacation and commuter traffic on narrow, beat-up roads presented one last challenge. This was about as bad as it got on the entire trip—shoulder-less roads, construction, and overzealous motorists were also to blame. Traffic was bumper to bumper in both directions. With absolutely no shoulder, we carved out space in the travel lane. Potholes and old cracked pavement made navigation and consistent steering difficult.

Under the circumstances, it was nearly impossible to ride in a straight line, which apparently annoyed trailing motorists. When one motorist shouted a profanity at Debbie, the travel experience had hit an all-time low. Eventually, we cleared the congestion, bringing the end of our trip into clear view.

Debbie couldn't wait to see the Atlantic, but we needed to travel north along the coast for a few miles before the ceremonial toe-dipping. The last beautiful spot was, of course, the Atlantic Ocean, at the end of our awesome trip. The deep blue Atlantic, with its crashing waves and rocky coastline, was a welcome sight and naturally reminded us we had arrived "home!"

Just landed!

Over the years, many have modified Emerson's famous quotation, "Life is a journey, not a destination." We agree with one such modification, "The joy is in the journey, not in the destination." But how much joy would we have missed had we shortened the journey? This day's arrival at

Dick Roderick's was a prime example. Surrounded by a handful of significant well-wishers prepared to sprinkle a bit of frosting on our delicious escapade, the joy, thrill, and satisfaction of finishing, and finishing well, could not be contained on our exuberant faces. Goals are made not only to strive for, but also to achieve.

Sharing success with those you love is special. Our family and friends are scattered all over the country. Nevertheless, we felt a deep sense of connection with, and appreciation for, those from afar who loved, encouraged, and supported us along the way. Your emotional presence in our lives helps to complete them.

Quick Turnaround

After pictures, cleaning up, warm conversation, and a satisfying meal, Richard Sirois, my college roommate, transported us to Massachusetts. While Debbie went to bed in anticipation of her first day of work several hours later, Richard and I stayed up until two thirty in the morning talking. We had so much to discuss. When I went to bed, there was Debbie, in bed, but wide-eyed awake. The excitement made sleeping a virtual impossibility. With little to no sleep, she couldn't wait to go to school and see everyone. There was so much to tell.

11. Simplicity

WE EXPERIENCED A PRECIOUS SIMPLICITY to life on the road. Debbie and I embarked on an adventure to break out of our humdrum lives and see God's beauty along the way. Our simple goal was to ride as far as we could, if not all of the way across the continent, while enjoying one another and the experience. We brought just the bare necessities: clothing, tools of our trade, and the means to acquire food and shelter. Our responsibility was one of diligence. We learned how to accomplish our objectives along the way, thanks to the advice of others and our own life experiences. Our needs were met daily without knowing the details in advance.

We had to establish an effective system and set certain boundaries to prevent external distractions from impeding progress. Spending too much time with extraneous matters, even though they might otherwise have been beneficial or enjoyable, was counterproductive. There were trade-offs; some might even refer to them as sacrifices. We had limited time to reach out personally to family and friends. We passed on opportunities to visit attractions and to converse with more people from different parts of the country.

Our simple goals provided direction. Our "life system" consisted of eating appropriately, exercising regularly, getting sufficient sleep, spending regular time on spiritual matters, and maintaining our clothing and equipment. The result of pursuing straightforward objectives and respecting healthy boundaries was to reap the reward: enjoying God's blessings along the way. The most profound of those blessings was to share the experience with one another, reawakening to a more diverse world than our prior daily routines availed us. Integral to this blessing was bonding as husband and wife, getting to know and love one another more each day of the journey. The icing on the cake was to make it all the way to the Atlantic Ocean!

During two months of life on the road, we discovered we were just fine if we missed the evening news and the business report.

The price of oil, politics in the local school system, or global unrest was meaningless. For that matter, other concerns beyond our control were not worth getting upset or worrying about. It did not matter whether the Red Sox were winning. We survived, in fact thrived, without the morning paper, haircuts, yard work, televised sports, political talk shows, new carpet in the living room, visiting the chiropractor, home improvement projects, manicures, facials, or counselors. These things are not wrong, just not that important in the grand scheme. Undistracted, we were free to enjoy God's wonderful creation. We found like-minded people along the way who were also enjoying it. Those who chose not to were best left to their own misery.

Life on the road was a fresh start of sorts. Far removed from our two-month episode were life's problems: bills landing in the mail, difficult people, job demands, the cares of this world. Some would say a cross-country bicycle trip is not a realistic existence. Who could argue with that? However, to dismiss this adventure and return to life as usual would have been to miss something very profound. We had a unique opportunity to unplug from the old life and plug into a new life, such as it was, and learn how to build a meaningful existence in our new little world. Without the distractions and disruptions that typically plagued our daily lives, we could gain better perspective and reassess what was truly important.

Life on the road was also a case study of sorts. Are there not some principles from the bike trip applicable to everyday life? What is our purpose for being alive? What interests, abilities, passions, and gifts do we have? How can we use these to fulfill our purpose? What goals can we set that will move us closer to achieving our purpose? What boundaries on our relationships and our time are appropriate to achieve these goals? Is it time for a fresh start in "real" life?

We (Debbie and I, and yes, you!) now have an opportunity to reinvent the old life. How much "stuff" do we really need? We did not need much on the bike trip. In fact, we had to jettison excess baggage in order to make the trip easier and more enjoyable. What activities are worthwhile? On the bike trip, they were clearly those activities that contributed to the overriding goal. Other activities only bogged us down. How are we allocating our time? What should our priorities be? On the bike trip, these decisions were self-evident given our objectives.

Let's face it, when you get to middle age, you are thinking about winding down, planning for those days when you can't get out of bed. You may have seen your parents struggle with aging and you can see it around the corner in your own life. Debbie and I are here to tell you it doesn't have to be that way. There is plenty of life to be lived after fifty, and you live it with the advantage of life experience and wisdom. But don't waste any more time thinking about it. Grab life by the horns and ride it for all you can. You are called to make a difference with what has already been entrusted to you.

Unlike a cross-country bike trip, appropriate life goals may not be self-evident. However, striving for simplicity will help in identifying and achieving them. Here are some keys we have learned navigating through life. Our story reflects them well. It helps to share needs with supportive family, friends, and professionals who have more experience and who can offer a unique perspective. It also helps to have an effective filter to test advice from others, assess personal motives, and set appropriate goals. Debbie and I use what we have learned from the Bible, a time-tested book that reveals truth—truth that can set one free. The Bible is an effective moral compass. Lastly, there is no substitute for life experience—it pays to remember lessons learned the hard way.

A healthy life has balance on a multitude of fronts. Going too deep in one area, like work, will cause other areas, like family, community, recreation, and spirituality, to suffer. It is easier than ever to get out of balance. How does one get in, and stay in, balance? The first step is to know what a healthy life looks like and to visualize how one's unique personality can thrive on multiple fronts. The second is to establish goals that will actualize one's vision. Pure motives, consistent with one's moral compass, will help establish a worthy destination. Money is often a barometer in setting goals, but not often the best one. Will these goals emphasize one's unique

God-given gifts and passions? What are you about? What is your life plan? If you have a plan, do your activities mesh with it?

It is difficult to describe what it meant for Debbie and me to journey on the bicycle trip together. Bicycling coast to coast was just one of many life activities that would not be possible, or certainly not as enjoyable, without that special someone alongside. And, now, of course, we journey through life together. Our union has launched us into a new world filled with adventure, opening the doorway for deeper experiences, character growth and refinement, and explosive opportunity for God to use us. A caring smile, an understanding heart, a passionate kiss and a warm hug, kind and gentle words, insightful advice, or simply a helping hand are now just an earshot away. The all-in-one package of camaraderie, companionship, and deeply intimate love has been well worth the wait. And our capacity to fill these roles expands as we grow closer every day.

If you are still waiting for your lifelong companion, Debbie and I encourage you not to lose hope. We also encourage you not to settle for second best. God wants to give you your heart's desire in His perfect timing. We know, we know! Sometimes, it feels like it is never going to happen. We thought that for thirty years. But history shows it has happened, it does happen, and it will happen! As you wait, God is pouring into you more and more character, preparing you for the appointed time and the appointed one. So, reject those feelings of despair, inadequacy, depression, and loneliness. Enjoy the blessings you have been given for a season. And continue to trust the pull of your soul that tells you that two are better. Your instincts are correct.

Our bike adventure was a special gift from God, a time of celebration, cleansing, reassessing, and reflection, a springboard to getting "unstuck" from a life built through repetition and held together by nothing more than inertia and insecurity. We believe that new seasons in life can bring joy, happiness, and fulfillment. It is time to build a new, intentional life and make it stick! Faith and courage will help jump-start us.

Between the lines of this book, there is a lesson about life. Life on the road was a microcosm of a simpler time and a simpler life.

Sometimes, we just make life way too complicated. Today's fast-paced culture, with its technology, progressive thinking, and competitive nature, can entangle the unsuspecting. A fresh start is available to anyone, any day, anywhere in our land of freedom and opportunity. You can reinvent yourself and your life if you have the will and insight to do so. We hope to see you on the trail!

Are you stuck in a rut? Dreams are special. Like a dash of salt on bland food, dreams can make life come alive. If you are contemplating your own grand dream, we encourage you to keep the dream alive, feed it regularly, and begin planning for it today. It will change your life. Debbie and I bought the largest digital picture frame we could find for our living room and run a continuous slideshow of our bike trip on a regular basis. Not a day goes by without reminiscing about some aspect of our adventure. You will do the same! Completing your own adventure is a gift from God that you will carry with you the rest of your life.

Debbie and I began our journey—well, both journeys for that matter—as complete novices. Yet, we were able to learn, grow, and experience great joy as we pursued our passion. We hope our story inspires you to action. No matter what your dream is, the same principles apply. What if you only had six months to live? How would you choose to spend your remaining days? Nurture your dream and take steps to realize it today. Do not let this opportunity pass you by—you are not getting any younger.

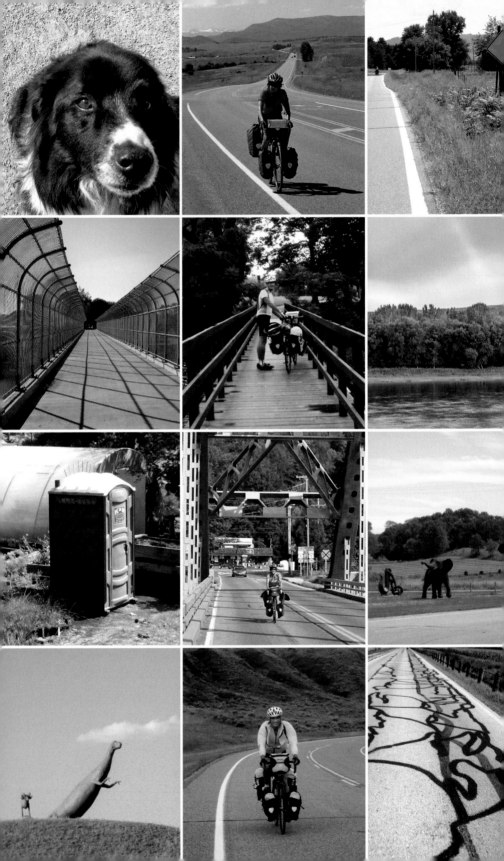

Epilogue

JUST AS YOU DISCOVERED when reading our story, much can happen in a short period. We weren't a day inside our home after our bicycle adventure before Debbie suggested another bicycle trip the following summer. But early in 2011, I mysteriously developed a blood clot in my right leg. Going from being in the best shape of my life to lying on my back 24/7 was not much fun and certainly not what I was expecting from married life. Neither was Debbie. Her care, however, was spectacular, attesting to the truth of *Two Are Better*. The seeds for this book project took root during my prolonged recuperation. It seemed like an ideal time to begin penning our thoughts with memories fresh in our minds. A year after the blood clot, I have no physical restrictions and am rebuilding my strength and stamina for what we hope to be future bicycle touring.

Meanwhile, Debbie's father, Dick Trapp, has made a remarkable recovery since his fall after our wedding. In 2011, after many months of rehab, he progressed from a nursing home facility back to assisted living.

In early 2012, after several months of up-and-down health requiring some onsite support, my mother, Frannie Bishop, passed away. She lived a wonderful and long life, and was a woman of great faith and consistency. I was able to spend much one-on-one time with her before Debbie came into my life. I feel extremely grateful for the blessing of her presence, love, example, and wisdom in my life for over half a century.

These events drive home a primary theme of this book: you only have so long to do what you are called to do. You don't know when your window of opportunity will slam shut for good. So, get at it! Debbie and I are convinced now, more than ever, that two are better than one. Since our trip, we have continued to grow together, with God's help, as one. While doing so, God continues to refine our character and prepare us for what He has in store.

We are hopeful *Two Are Better* urges you on toward new life adventures. We would love to hear how it has. Please contact us at www.openroadpress.com to let us know. Thanks for reading, and may God richly bless your adventures.

Trip Log

Date	Destination	Accommodations	Miles	Cum. Miles	Avg. Speed	Max Speed	Min Elev.	Max Elev.	Elev. Gain	Elev. Loss	Cal. Burn
Starting in	Seaside, OR	The Masseys'									
July 3	Westport, OR	Motel	47	47	10.2	33.0	-17	630	2,648	2,628	2,450
July 4	Portland, OR	Motel	72	119	11.5	34.5	126	893	2,026	2,023	3,605
July 5	Cascade Locks, OR	Motel	55	174	10.7	27.2	-9	854	2,087	2,054	3,329
July 6	Biggs, OR	Motel	66	240	9.6	30.5	-49	595	2,965	2,896	3,520
July 7	Crow Butte, WA	Camping	57	297	8.6	28.3	186	1,009	1,954	1,864	2,087
July 8	Umatilla, OR	Motel	37	334	10.3	24.2	269	453	908	754	1,506
July 9	Walla Walla, WA	Motel	54	388	11.9	24.4	373	1,021	1,253	760	2,420
July 10	Clarkston, WA	Motel	96	484	11.9	41.3	740	2,739	4,285	4,459	4,232
July 11	Cul de Sac, ID	Camping	40	524	7.6	30.0	797	3,554	3,820	1,101	2,364
July 12	Kamiah, ID	Motel	54	578	12.3	36.6	1,308	4,172	2,322	4,567	2,126
July 13	Clearwater Nat For, ID	Camping	55	633	10.7	NMF	1,318	2,154	1,650	826	3,000
July 14	Lolo Hot Springs, MT	Motel	60	693	10.6	28.7	2,076	5,171	3,377	1,349	4,749
July 15	Missoula, MT	Motel	38	731	14.2	28.6	3,194	4,252	324	1,267	1,721
July 16	Lincoln, MT	Motel	78	809	12.5	30.8	3,074	4,417	2,873	1,537	3,936
July 17	Great Falls, MT	Motel	88	897	11.2	32.3	3,415	5,724	3,111	4,254	3,644
July 18-21	Great Falls, MT	Motel	Rest	897							
July 22	Fort Benton, MT	Motel	55	952	11.9	41.7	2,602	3,668	1,921	2,592	2,385
July 23	Havre, MT	Motel	73	1,025	11.5	30.4	2,439	3,030	1,342	1,520	3,055
July 24	Malta, MT	Motel	88	1,113	12.2	27.6	2,132	2,438	701	928	3,656
July 25	Glasgow, MT	Motel	70	1,183	13.3	28.8	2,023	2,367	1,216	1,353	3,031
July 26	Poplar, MT	Motel	71	1,254	13.1	26.2	2,030	2,338	747	884	3,089
July 27	Williston, ND	The Hegstads'	81	1,335	12.3	29.3	1,905	2,399	1,852	1,929	3,469
July 28	Shuttle to Minot, ND	The Hegstads'	Rest	1,335							
July 29	Rugby, ND	Motel	60	1,395	12.1	26.2	1,482	1,691	494	608	2,469
July 30	Carrington, ND	Motel	98	1,493	14.9	28.6	1,578	1,839	1,441	1,404	4,680
July 31	Mayville, ND	Camping	93	1,586	13.7	35.2	937	1,626	942	1,601	4,100
August 1	Fargo, ND	Motel	60	1,646	12.0	21.9	842	969	223	275	2,498
August 2	Fergus Falls, MN	Motel	79	1,725	12.4	23.9	887	1,405	1,765	1,414	3,484
August 3	Long Prairie, MN	Motel	83	1,808	13.5	28.0	1,250	1,705	1,807	1,722	3,822
August 4	Foreston, MN	The Shultses'	69	1,877	14.2	31.9	1,049	1,407	1,093	1,248	3,204
August 5	Shuttle:Wabasha, MN	The Aaslands'	Rest	1,877							

August 6	Winona, MN	The Porters'	40	1,917	14.1	25.8	741	817	618	614	1,833
August 7	Shuttle: Cascade, IA	The Porters'	Rest	1,917							
August 8	Wilton, IA	Motel	61	1,978	11.2	24.1	723	1,035	2,317	2,462	2,564
August 9	Kewanee, IL	Motel	90	2,068	12.5	28.5	154	752	2,252	2,528	3,926
August 10	Streator, IL	Motel	69	2,137	12.4	26.7	657	1,118	1,419	1,646	2,994
August 11	Kankakee, IL	The Linnemans'	70	2,207	14.7	29.4	838	981	704	709	3,384
August 12	Rensselaer, IN	Motel	53	2,260	13.0	20.2	533	687	458	430	2,412
August 13	Wabash, IN	Motel	87	2,347	12.3	21.8	551	823	1,398	1,221	3,690
August 14	Monroeville, IN	Camping	60	2,407	14.0	28.4	685	854	941	922	2,809
August 15	Napoleon, OH	Motel	67	2,474	13.7	21.8	639	805	586	705	3,070
August 16	Milan, OH	Motel	94	2,568	14.1	22.8	685	806	801	860	4,400
August 17	Cleveland, OH	Motel	51	2,619	13.8	22.7	540	636	609	621	2,409
August 18	Cleveland, OH	Motel	Rest	2,619							
August 19	Conneaut, OH	Motel	91	2,710	12.8	27.2	359	886	2,019	1,553	4,465
August 20	Westfield, NY	Motel	67	2,777	11.6	27.1	690	877	1,667	1,662	3,140
August 21	Hamburg, NY	Motel	62	2,839	12.3	26.3	369	649	1,629	1,540	2,896
August 22	Niagara Falls, ON	Motel	45	2,884	11.5	22.4	368	799	859	977	2,072
August 23	Medina, NY	Motel	49	2,933	11.6	27.1	475	697	1,124	1,217	2,237
August 24	Egypt, NY	Motel	61	2,994	11.7	25.7	494	709	1,025	1,083	2,846
August 25	Fulton, NY	Motel	78	3,072	11.8	32.6	305	668	3,398	3,533	3,603
August 26	Redfield, NY	Motel	47	3,119	12.2	30.3	223	1,091	2,155	1,470	2,331
August 27	Raquette Lake, NY	Motel	79	3,198	11.9	32.0	720	1,664	4,374	3,616	4,591
August 28	Ticonderoga, NY	Motel	86	3,284	12.2	35.5	259	2,176	4,605	6,046	4,709
August 29	Middlebury, VT	Motel	25	3,309	9.2	30.5	133	542	1,793	1,619	1,324
August 30	Fairlee, VT	Motel	75	3,384	10.9	35.0	417	2,154	4,979	5,003	4,641
August 31	Conway, NH	Motel	77	3,461	11.6	41.2	433	2,859	4,804	4,765	4,472
September 1	Cape Elizabeth, ME	Home: Marlborough, MA	68	3,529	12.3	33.6	-25	545	2,322	2,866	3,328
53 Days	15 States and Canada	Total	3,529						100,003	99,485	167,777
		Average	67		12.2	29.0	942	1,701	1,969	1,989	3,362
		Maximum	98		14.9	41.7	3,415	5,724	4,979	6,046	4,749
		Minimum	25		7.6	20.2	-49	453	223	275	1,324

■ Maximum
□ Minimum

— Minimum elevation represents the lowest elevation achieved and is expressed as estimated feet above sea level as determined by bicycle computer. Maximum elevation represents the highest level.

— Elevation gained is a measure of feet climbed and elevation lost is a measure of feet descended.

— Calories burned are also estimated by the bicycle computer, which was not calibrated for the load weight.

Acknowledgments

We would like to thank the following individuals, who were instrumental in making *Two Are Better* come to fruition.

By providing critical input into preliminary drafts of *Two Are Better*: Bonnie Mikoski, Dave Aldrich, David Zelz, Dick Roderick, Erin Casey, Foster and MaryJane Williams, Frannie Bishop, Glen Stairs, Janet Timmins, Jill Hoyt, John David Kudrick, Kathy McHenry, Ken Goodin, Mark Gries, Mark Orrin, Paul Hoyt, Randall Burns, and Scott Emack.

By providing logistical support on the trip itself: Chris Brown, Chuck and Melinda Shults, Danny Ricciotti, Dick and Patti Roderick, Glen Stairs, Jennifer Aasland, Jim and Karen Massey, Loisanne Ross, Matt Bishop, Mike and Anne Porter, Mike and Wendy Kulik, Mike Hartley (from Maine Sport Outfitters), Randy and Marilynn Bishop, Richard Sirois, Steve (owner of Tern of the Wheel) and Joan Linneman, Tim and Laurie Hegstad, and Wayne Boroughs (from thetouringstore.com).

Special thanks to Jim and Karen Massey, who hosted us on our first two days on the West Coast. Jim was so helpful with advice, encouragement, transporting us to the ocean, and providing nutritional products courtesy of his company, Mountain Peak Nutritionals.

Special thanks to Richard Sirois, whose late-night service transporting us back to Massachusetts at the end of our trip got Debbie back to work.

The novelty of our adventure universally elicited earnest support. A successful bicycle tour and a fulfilling journey through life are dependent upon input from others with more expertise and experience. Thanks to all who have helped make our trips so enjoyable.

TheHopeLine

1-800-394-HOPE (4673)

thehopeline.com

God continues to bless us with a rewarding stockpile of personal conversations with downtrodden youth on TheHopeLine. TheHopeLine is a help service that seeks to reach and rescue hurting teens and young adults. Trained Hope Coaches handle phone calls and Internet chats from youth in crisis, and seek to listen, encourage, apply Scripture, and pray for their issues. Hope Coaches will refer these youth to partner agencies that offer expertise with issues such as suicide, addiction, and abuse.

TheHopeLine, part of the Dawson McAllister Association, has transformed many lives since its inception in 1989. Although it deals with a wide array of youth issues, the organization claims to have intervened in over 1,200 potential suicides in 2011 alone. McAllister, a dynamic youth speaker and author who has been in youth ministry since the 1970s, hosts a live, call-in radio show, *DMLive*, syndicated on Top-40 stations nationwide to connect teens and young adults with the nonprofit's services. Their website offers a multitude of resources for healing hurts. The association partners with like-minded organizations that provide additional services, including counselors and e-mail mentors.

Debbie and I have personally witnessed the difference that God's power and love have made in youth with whom we've interacted on TheHopeLine. We are honored to serve as volunteer Hope Coaches.

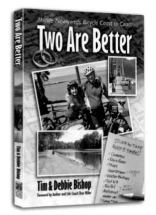